WHEN SCIENCE
GOES WRONG

WHEN SCIENCE GOES WRONG

The Desire and Search for Truth

Guy Consolmagno, SJ, and
Christopher M. Graney

Vatican Observatory

Paulist Press
New York / Mahwah, NJ

Cover photo by Oleksandr Pidvalnyi / Pexels.com
Cover design by Joe Gallagher
Book design by Lynn Else

Library of Congress Cataloging-in-Publication Data
is available upon request.

ISBN 978-0-8091-5664-1 (paperback)
ISBN 978-0-8091-8825-3 (e-book)

Published by Paulist Press
997 Macarthur Boulevard
Mahwah, New Jersey 07430
www.paulistpress.com

Printed and bound in the
United States of America

Contents

List of Illustrations

Chapter 1

Chapter 2

Chapter 3

Chapter 4

Foreword

An essential part of contemporary conversations on science, faith, and theology is having a grasp of what is going on not only in religious belief and theology but also in scientific method, discovery, and practice.

The authors of this readable study are astronomers at the Vatican Observatory in Castel Gandolfo, Italy. Lovers of science themselves, they show us how science can go wrong and where it has veered from rightness both intellectually and morally. I find the book helpful in its generous display of instances where modern science, especially astronomy, has had to undergo constant transformation despite its most noble attempts at accuracy.

While reading the manuscript, I could not help looking at its investigations in the light of what I consider to be the most philosophically impressive study of scientific understanding available, the book *Insight: A Study of Human Understanding* by the Jesuit philosopher and theologian Bernard Lonergan. First published in the late 1950's, *Insight* remains a towering intellectual achievement as relevant now as ever. It sets forth strict criteria as to how to measure the integrity of scientific claims, and it also shows its readers how to distinguish scientific theory from commonsense understanding. *When Science Goes Wrong* provides many useful examples that Lonergan himself might have chosen in showing how science (or should I say scientists?) have gone wrong.

WHEN SCIENCE GOES WRONG

While the Vatican Observatory was continuing to gain recognition and respect, Lonergan was teaching and writing nearby at the Gregorian University in Rome where he worked out a brilliant theory of knowledge using science as his model. He showed how, in the history of science and philosophical thought, great thinkers have strayed time and again from the human mind's disinterested desire to know and from a proper understanding of truth and objectivity. Lonergan's work can still instruct us on how to distinguish experience from understanding, seeing from knowing, and bright ideas from true ideas. *Insight* and subsequent writings of Lonergan have demonstrated how the life of the mind must not become independent of the life of virtue and (especially in his later writings) how "objectivity is the fruit of authentic subjectivity."

And he showed how "bias" suppresses the human desire to be attentive, insightful, truthful, self-critical, and responsible. The authors of the present book, providing an ample number of examples, are also especially sensitive to how bias and unexamined assumptions lead our minds astray, including the minds of scientists. If I were teaching Lonergan's thought in a college classroom today, I would find in the chapters of this book lively illustrations of how bias (especially confirmation bias) has affected the modern history of science.

This readable book is intended to be popular rather than academically formal. It does occasionally dip into the larger question of the relationship of science to faith, religion, and theology, but the authors keep their modest reflections on this heated set of issues mostly on the back burner. Nevertheless, the book serves its purpose by providing a considerable amount of material that could be used fruitfully in introductory classes on science and religion, the history of science, and even the philosophy of science, at least as supplemental reading.

Where Science Goes Wrong is, I should add, testimony to the authors' own exemplary concern for rightness of thought, faith, and action.

John F. Haught
Distinguished Research Professor of Theology
Georgetown University

Introduction

Sometimes Science Goes Wrong

Br. Guy first met Nancy about thirty years ago. She was a single mother whose teenage daughter Julie had a lively interest in astronomy. Over the years, he watched Julie grow up, enter a career in medical technology, marry a sweet young guy, and start her own family. Today, Julie has two daughters who remind Br. Guy of Julie when she was a teenager. Nancy sends him regular updates on the adventures of her grandchildren.

During December 2021, the grandkids spent their free time in a hospital room, reading to their father, while he drifted in and out of a coma. It was COVID-19. Soon after Christmas, their father died. Among his final words to his daughters, he apologized that he had not gotten vaccinated.

It's a story that played out too many times around the world during the COVID-19 pandemic. The stubborn refusal by good and smart people to accept the vaccine is one of the especially tragic elements of those stories.

"Follow the science!" had been the rallying cry of those who promoted vaccination. But as a slogan, it clearly did not work. And, tragic as that death was, there was just enough truth behind the fear of vaccines that one can understand why good, smart people could be skeptical. Sometimes science gets it wrong.

WHEN SCIENCE GOES WRONG

This book is a collection of stories from history about science getting it wrong. Often, science going wrong makes for amusing stories. And sometimes, especially when the science is not about remote things like stars or the moons of Jupiter, but about people—like during the pandemic—the stories are tragic, not amusing.

Amusing or not, the stories in this book are ones that we, the authors, think are valuable. They can help us all to understand what science is (and isn't), and how it is possible for human beings to "follow" the science to some very wrong conclusions—by extrapolating too far beyond what we know, by mashing up ideas, by forgetting our biases, by failing in our imaginations, and by fixating on certain preconceptions. When we think that following science is a sure way to get to all the right answers, we misunderstand the nature and history of science.

The authors of this book have some experience in dealing with misunderstandings about science in the public realm, misunderstandings about what we are trying to do in our labs and with our telescopes. We are both professionals and popularizers in our fields of astronomy and the history of astronomy. Folks who want to keep up to date will always ask us, "What's the latest?" But in fact, "the latest" in science is the very stuff that's most likely going to be wrong—and of course, that's what makes it so exciting!

The misunderstanding comes, in part, from how people learn science. In most introductory science classes, science is presented as a problem-solving system. Do you want to pass the test? Then your answers had better match what is in the answer key. But those are just exercises to develop in a student the habit of thinking the way a scientist thinks. They are not science any more than playing scales is the same thing as playing music.

Real science is the process of figuring out things where we don't know the answers...or where the answers that we thought we knew are only *almost* correct. As a system of knowledge, science is always incomplete—by design. Progress means making our old textbooks—and answer keys—obsolete or incorrect.

Yet still, at any given moment, in many parts of our lives—such as medicine—science represents the best we can know.

A theologian knows that every heresy is based on an important truth: even ideas that ultimately are incorrect gain traction because they are based on at least a grain of truth, a truth that truly does matter even if it is not the whole truth. This is the case with skepticism regarding the vaccine, and science in general. There is a grain of truth behind vaccine skepticism. Vaccines do not have a perfect history. Side effects to the vaccination process are common, and they can vary in severity from case to case. Safety and efficacy are issues that require a long period of study before approving a vaccine for general use; and even with that lengthy process, mistakes can and do happen.

For individual cases, the occasion can arise where the worst fears of the antivaccine community do come true. Some individual deaths following the use of one of the COVID-19 vaccines were attributed to blood clots associated with that vaccine; the use of one promising, easy-to-administer vaccine was subsequently curtailed. Meanwhile, the financial incentives for approving new vaccines and new drugs can warp even the most careful system of safety approval. Thousands of adults today still carry the birth defects caused by thalidomide, which had been hoped to be a safe aid for morning sickness and thus widely prescribed to pregnant women in Europe in the 1960s.

At the same time, outlandish claims about the power of science and technology from people who want to encourage us to follow the best medical advice ironically give credence to the outlandish fears certain people have of microchips or mind-control drugs hidden in those vaccines.

But none of this invalidates the value of vaccines, or medicine, or science in general. And all this amounts to little more

WHEN SCIENCE GOES WRONG

than clever debating points. Meanwhile, the granddaughters of Br. Guy's friend have lost their father, a death that didn't have to occur.

During the COVID-19 pandemic, many people thought that science had gone wrong...and, insofar as it became a subject of political tribalism and cultural identity, resulting in sickness and death that didn't have to occur, it did go wrong. It failed to be that agreed-upon source of truth that people expected it to be.

In fact, science is not so good at being an agreed-upon source of truth, even if it represents the best we can know. Sure, science tells us that gravity holds the moon in its orbit and causes apples to fall from trees; it tells us that salt is a combination of sodium and chlorine; that the sun will rise tomorrow because the Earth, which is a sphere, rotates; that the COVID-19 pandemic was caused by a microscopic thing, hardly even alive, called a virus. These things are true. Perhaps they are not quite the same level of truth as *pi = 3.14159265...*, or as a straight line touching a circle at a maximum of two points, but you can surely bet the house on them.

We honor the giants of science who gave us gravity (F = Gm_1m_2/r^2) and salt (NaCl) as "the people who got things right." But science is not all gravity or salt. And in fact, while we rightly honor those scientific giants of the past, in truth, they weren't always right.

We astronomers think of Aristotle, Galileo, Kepler, and others, whom you will encounter in the chapters of this book, as being giants who, to borrow the words of Isaac Newton, let us see farther by standing on their shoulders. But realizing that the giants weren't always right doesn't make them any less giants. And after all, when was the last time you tried standing on someone's shoulders? It can be a precarious perch up there! You had better learn how to land gracefully if—no, when—you fall off. We learn about science not only when we learn about what its giants could show us, but also when we see where its giants, and those standing on their shoulders, went wrong.

Science is so much more than just taking a measuring tool like a ruler to the world and gathering quantitative, reproducible data. Like all sciences, astronomy is not merely recording facts; it's that very human attempt at understanding those facts.

Think about the actual day-to-day work of an astronomer: for every hour we spend at a telescope, getting data, getting facts, we spend many more hours thinking about how those facts fit into what we thought we knew before and what we are puzzled about at the moment. It's reading the scientific papers written by other astronomers; writing our own papers for them to read; attending meetings where we can hear the latest ideas from each other and share the most recent data; and having conversations with each other late at night over our beverage of choice. Astronomy is more than the study of stars and planets: it is the study of how we human beings go about trying to understand those data about stars and planets. Astronomy, even when much of it is done alone at a telescope or in front of a computer screen, is ultimately a social, human activity.

And it's not just an activity with our colleagues of today. We also join up with the community of the past, conversing with the astronomers who went before us, whose writings have preserved the conversations of their times. After all, before we attempt to chime into any conversation, it's only polite to pay attention to what others before us have said. Indeed, it is necessary to listen before we talk if we want to make a useful contribution. Without listening to the past, we won't appreciate what it was they were trying to say, or understand how they went wrong—much less, get their jokes!

The scientists who got it wrong in the past were part of the conversations of their times. And by "got it wrong," we do not mean the crackpots who do not know what science really is. We mean those scientists who were *almost* correct, whose ideas were scientifically reasonable at the time. Even while our data and concepts today have gone beyond those of past scientists, what we do today is built on their insights and their mistakes—on their shoulders.

So, in this book, we are going to introduce you to some stories of mistakes from the history of science:

- In chapter 1, we will take you on a quick tour of the ever-changing ideas scientists have had about our universe over the last 2500 years: What are the stars? What is the Earth? Is it a special place, and what does that mean for us?
- In chapter 2, we will introduce a not-so-ancient view of our Earth that we think will amaze and delight you: a world of bottomless seas, raging waters, and the ever-present hand of God. Oh yes, there was scientific thinking involved in all that, too.
- In chapter 3, you will meet some brilliant scientists, thinking brilliant scientific thoughts that were two centuries ahead of their time. They were *right*. Except...they were not right in the way they would have wanted.
- In chapter 4, you will find that even though Harry Potter himself has had some strange ideas about the moons of Jupiter, his wild misunderstanding could not top the stranger ideas of real astronomers.

These stories are amazing and amusing. Along with Harry Potter, Mark Twain's Captain Stormfield makes an appearance—and intelligent beings from other planets, of course. Even Bigfoot shows up!

Introduction: Sometimes Science Goes Wrong

But science going wrong is not always amusing. Sometimes people who have been crucial to science's progress get left out of our common stories. But worse, sometimes when science goes wrong, people don't just get forgotten—they get badly hurt. In chapter 5, you will hear what can happen when science is used to put a value on human beings. It is not amusing. It is, however, an undeniable part of science's history.

Science going wrong is not just something confined to history. Here's a shocking truth: ultimately, the point of our science, even today, is *not* to come up with the "right answer." Now, that can be a problem when everyone is turning to science for the Right Answer, for the truth, as they did during the pandemic. But both as scientists and as human beings, we know that sometimes we learn the most by encountering ideas that challenge us to realize that we don't have that answer.

Isaac Asimov is often quoted as having said, "The most exciting phrase to hear in science is not 'Eureka' but 'hmm...that's funny....'" In other words, not "I have got it!" but rather, "Oh, wait, I don't have it...that doesn't look right." When we say, "That can't be right; so, where did it go wrong?" we gain a greater insight into what we do believe, and what it really means, than if we just keep trying to convince ourselves we were right all along.

Saying "That can't be right" implies change. Science involves change. Our datasets grow, our theories get replaced, our very cosmologies change. Philosophy may lay claim to eternal truths. Mathematics certainly does—the value of *pi* or the number of points where a line intersects a circle qualify as unchanging truths. But in science, what we believe to be true today has changed from what we believed to be true a couple of decades—or centuries—ago.

That's why we don't teach today's science classes using old textbooks. In the future, some of our ideas today will be seen as having been *almost* correct and will not be in the textbooks. Indeed, our science is strengthened by experiencing change, and by being confronted with what went wrong. That's where we find out what's essential—what might be true, even—and what is cultural baggage.

Looking back through history, and looking at science today, those who move science forward are not always those who have the latest techniques or the fastest computers or the loudest voices claiming to have the right answers. More often, they are the ones with the best imaginations, those willing to put the data together in new and creative ways. They're the ones who do not merely help answer the age-old questions; they are the ones who suggest new questions and know how to get the rest of the field excited by those questions.

And here's the most important part, and why people of faith should care about understanding how science comes to the truth. Showing that science can be wrong is not merely some way of justifying "faith" instead of "science." In fact, that's the exact opposite of our message. Rather, seeing how science grows ever closer to the truth by recognizing where and how it goes wrong, we can learn in just the same way how to grow in our understanding of God, who is truth itself. The worst kind of wrong is to be self-satisfied with what we think we already know and stop seeking to be ever closer to God.

Because even as we learn more, the essential questions remain constant: Who are we? Where did we come from? What are we doing here? These are questions that science can help address, especially the fields of astronomy and cosmology. But ultimately, they are not questions to be answered with a number or an equation. And most certainly, they are not the sorts of questions that lead to the sorts of answers that everyone will agree are the right answers, to be found in the answer key. They are mysteries for contemplation. Going wrong is just part of the process.

And when you're dealing with mystery, recognizing when you're *almost* correct looks an awful lot like progress.

Chapter 1

The Stars and Us

Science takes what we observe and what we know (or think we know) about what we've seen, and from that, it attempts to draw general inferences about the universe. It tries to extract deeper principles from the things that are seen, to understand why things happen the way they do...and even to infer what must have happened to get us to where we are, and what's likely to happen next. A fundamental tool we use for doing this is "extrapolation."

We extrapolate all the time. It's just common sense. Imagine that you're traveling down a freeway with the cruise control set; you glance at the speedometer and see that it reads seventy miles per hour. A few minutes later, when you look at the speedometer, it's still reading seventy. So, you're probably not far wrong in assuming that you were going at seventy miles per hour a minute before you first looked, that you were going seventy between the two times you looked, and that you will still be going seventy a minute from now. Maybe somewhere in there the speed will be seventy-one or sixty-nine miles per hour, but close enough that the difference won't matter. Furthermore, if it is thirty-five miles to your exit, it is reasonable to suppose that you have half an hour of driving ahead of you.

WHEN SCIENCE GOES WRONG

Now, common sense also tells you that you can only take this so far. Sooner or later, you'll be coming to your exit, and then you'll want to slow down. If you hit a traffic snarl before that exit, it could take you much longer than half an hour to get there. If you don't have enough fuel in the tank, you could run out of gas and roll to a stop before you even get to the exit.

And a little bit of thought will make you realize that sometime in the past, somewhere, you must have started from a dead stop; and so there must have been a time when the car was accelerating up to speed. Indeed, there must even have been a time when there was no car, and no road, and maybe even no you to do the driving. Your simple extrapolation from how things are now, to how they used to be, or how they will be in the future, can't work forever. The trick with extrapolation is to know when you're extrapolating too far.

Perhaps the best illustration of how much things change in science, and go wrong by extrapolating too far, is our efforts over history to get at the big questions: Where did we come from? What is our place now? Where are we going? or Where did we first get on the highway? Where are we at this moment? And when is our exit coming up? That branch of science, what we call "cosmology," is our attempt to extrapolate from what we know about how the universe works now, to understand the structure and function of the universe itself everywhere, from beginning to end.

Every grade school child learns the basics of our cosmology. The Earth is a planet, a ball of rock circling the sun along with other planets like Venus and Jupiter. The sun is a star like billions of other stars in our galaxy, the Milky Way. And the Milky Way is one galaxy among billions of galaxies in the universe.

This picture seems rather uncomplicated—a reasonable cosmological Right Answer. But reaching this answer was not easy.

2

The first chapter of Genesis, written more than 2500 years ago, doesn't describe Earth as a planet alongside the other planets, or the sun as a star alongside the other stars:

> And God said, "Let there be a dome....Let there be lights in the dome of the sky...." God made the two great lights...and the stars. (Genesis 1:6, 14–16)

And yet Genesis is not horribly wrong. It does not promote a false picture of the universe. Why can we say that? For one thing, Genesis is not a book about the universe—it's a book about God. And, in fact, this book about the Creator does play an essential role in the way we understand creation. Even though the science it describes has been obsolete for thousands of years, Genesis is the book that makes science possible. It is the fundamental document on which all our science is based.

Genesis describes pretty much what we all can see even today when we look up, even as we know there's more to the universe than what we can see with our naked eye. In the way it describes the universe, Genesis assumes the same arrangement of the heavens and Earth that was postulated by the Babylonians, one of the leading civilizations of the time. They had conquered Jerusalem and carted off to Babylon the same Jewish intellectuals who ended up writing Genesis.

But the cosmological story of the Babylonians postulated that the creation of the physical universe occurred by accident, during a battle among deities; they taught that the high point of creation was the city of Babylon. By contrast, Genesis tells a very different story: the universe was created deliberately, on purpose, by the one God who is already there in the beginning—before the universe is created. It was all done in the light, nothing hidden. It happened as orderly as day follows night. And, at each step of the way, God saw that it was good. It's those differences from the Babylonian picture that are new and important. Those are the lessons that are still true today, regardless of your cosmology.

A universe as imagined by the Babylonians is not one that we could possibly generalize into physical laws. How could you extrapolate general principles from the chaos of a battle, or the whims of inscrutable gods? But Genesis describes a universe that is good, understandable, and ordered: a universe that is both orderly enough that you can extrapolate from the trends you see in it, and good enough to be worthy of study. (There *is* a highway, and it's worth driving down.)

Also notice that the Genesis version of creation depicts a universe that begins, and changes over time, without being trapped in a deterministic endless cycle. (The road is not just a big loop; it actually goes someplace.) This was a point of view very different from that of other surrounding cultures, like the Babylonians or the ancient civilizations of India.

Most importantly, Genesis holds up as the pinnacle of creation the Sabbath, the day of rest. Everything else that was created beforehand leads us to the moment when we can rest and appreciate it. (The place the road goes to is a place worth stopping at.) That gives us permission, and indeed encouragement, to rest from our daily tasks and reflect about the Creator...and of course God's creation. To do science.

The Babylonians could never have imagined the tools that we can use as scientists today to investigate the structure and nature of the universe. But even as our knowledge about what's in the universe grows, the questions remain the same. Does the universe have a beginning as Genesis says? Does it unfold linearly, or cyclically? Do we occupy a unique place within it?

Two centuries after the Babylonian captivity, Aristotle proposed a different picture of the universe from that of Genesis, even as he still assumed that we occupy a unique place in it. His idea of the physical universe was based on the notion that four elements make up our Earth: earth, water, air, fire. Each has a natural resting place; when displaced by some change, each element moves by its nature to get back to that resting place.

Meanwhile, he postulated that the remainder of the universe, the ever-present sun, moon, planets, stars—and the heavens that contain them all—is made of some mysterious unchanging stuff not found on Earth—a "fifth element," sometimes called "quintessence"—whose movement is powered by a single, unchanging god that Aristotle inferred must exist. (Interestingly, though we now recognize that the stars and planets we can see are, in fact, made of the same stuff as our home planet Earth, our modern observation of the universe, in light of the laws of physics as we currently understand them, demands that it is comprised mostly of "dark matter" and "dark energy"—mysterious stuff not easily found on Earth. Shades of Aristotle!)

Unlike the writer of Genesis, Aristotle believed that the universe had no beginning. Rather, he assumed it ran eternally through an endless cycle, linked to the motions of the planets through the circle of zodiac constellations. This concept also guided the ideas of the great Indian mathematician and astronomer Aryabhata. About eight hundred years after Aristotle, Aryabhata proposed that the stars were fixed in an unmoving sphere, and what we perceive as the daily rising and setting of the sun, stars, and other celestial objects is the evidence of the Earth turning in place. What is more, using data on planetary positions that he had inherited from the Greeks and Babylonians, he calculated the period of time it takes for the moon and visible planets to make one complete circuit of those stars, and his results were correct to a remarkable degree of accuracy.

But then he did an interesting thing; he extrapolated a cosmology from the different planets' periods.

Decimal points had not been developed by mathematicians then, so rather than say that the time required for one Martian circuit through the stars of the zodiac (as observed from Earth) is 2.135 Earth years, he could only say that in 427 Earth years Mars makes 200 circuits. And given ratios such as these for each planet, like astronomers before him going back to the Babylonians, he took the next obvious step of comparing all the ratios of all the planets (including the sun and moon) against a common period; he arrived at the number: four and a third billion years. That common period, assuming all the ratios of periods were exact and correct, would represent how long it would take for all the planets to repeat their positions. (Coincidentally, it is not that far from modern estimates of the age of the Earth and our solar system.)

Like Aristotle and many other cultures believed, ancient Hindu cosmology accepted the astrological idea that human and earthly events are controlled by the positions of the planets in the zodiac. If the planets repeat their positions every four and a third billion years, as extrapolation from the best astronomy of those days seemed to imply, and if those planetary positions controlled human events as they believed, then this calculation provided "solid scientific proof" that life on Earth was trapped in an endless cycle, relentlessly and inevitably repeating itself!

Alas, we now know that the orbits of planets are not perfect ratios, and there is no such common denominator to their various periods. But Aryabhata didn't know that; he couldn't have known that. His cyclic universe was a perfectly reasonable extrapolation from the patterns he saw, based on the best mathematics of his time. It just happened to be wrong. Not very wrong, in terms of a number—he pretty much got the Right Answer!—but wrong in making inferences about the universe by extrapolating beyond that number.

A few centuries before Aryabhata and about four centuries after Aristotle, the Greek-Egyptian astronomer Ptolemy

(~AD 150) used the observations of the Babylonians and Greeks to flesh out Aristotle's Earth-centered cosmology with mathematical rigor. Using geometry, he proved that the Earth was a tiny speck within the universe, with the stars immensely far away. He also provided mathematical tools that correctly— well, almost correctly—predicted the positions of the planets.

Of course, Ptolemy's universe was a far cry from the light-strewn dome described in Genesis. However, this radically different cosmology did not provoke a "religion and science" crisis within the still-young Christian world. Most theologians at that time saw in Ptolemy's physical cosmology (not unlike the cosmology of Aristotle) a reflection of the non-physical universe. St. Augustine in his *On the Literal Meaning of Genesis* (~AD 415) warned against citing Scripture over science: "Even a non-Christian knows something about the earth, the heavens, and the other elements of this world, about the motion and orbit of the stars...and this knowledge he holds to as being certain from reason and experience." Ptolemy's science was persuasive, and Augustine was concerned that if Christians stood against it with the cosmology of Genesis, that might make people less receptive to what Christians had to say about religious matters.

At one point, St. Augustine uses as an example how astronomers said that some stars were greater than the sun, and certainly than the moon, which Genesis 1:14–16 calls the "great lights" in the sky. This claim resulted from those immense distances Ptolemy had calculated: for the stars to appear the size they do in the night sky and be so far away, they must be very large indeed. By contrast, if sun, moon, and stars were all lights on a dome, the stars would be just as they appear—smaller than the sun and moon.

Ptolemaic astronomy contradicted a plain reading of Genesis regarding the relative sizes of the moon and stars. "Now, it is a disgraceful and dangerous thing for an infidel to hear a Christian," Augustine says, "presumably giving the meaning of Holy Scripture, talking nonsense on these topics." Genesis, he says, is describing the moon as it appears to our eyes, not making an absolute statement about its size. That sounds very modern. Of course, today the Ptolemaic science that he is citing has long been abandoned as being not even almost correct.

Fig. 1A. The relative sizes of the moon (left) and a star (right) according to Ptolemy. He determined that the moon in the night sky looks larger than the stars only because it is much, much closer than they are.

Augustine is not the only Christian saint who sounds modern yet cites Ptolemaic science. The universe of Ptolemy, not of Genesis, appears in St. Severinus Boethius's *Consolation of Philosophy*, a discussion on God and providence and evil that Boethius wrote from prison around the year AD 525. In considering the pursuit of glory, Boethius writes,

> Consider with me in the following detail, how limited this glory is! How frivolous and how contemptible! You have learned from astronomy, that this globe of earth is but as a point, in respect to the vast extent of the heavens; that is, the immensity of the celestial sphere is such that ours, when compared with it, is as nothing, and vanishes.

You know likewise, from the proofs that Ptolemy adduces, there is only one fourth part of this earth, which is of itself so small a portion of the universe, inhabited by creatures known to us. If from this fourth you deduct the space occupied by the seas and lakes, and the vast sandy regions which extreme heat and want of water render uninhabitable, there remains but a very small proportion of the terrestrial sphere for the habitation of men.

Enclosed then and locked up as you are, in an unperceivable point of a point, do you think of nothing but of blazing far and wide your name and reputation? What can there be great or pompous in a glory circumscribed in so narrow a circuit?

Boethius's works were widely read in medieval times, viewed as second in importance only to Aristotle and Augustine. Indeed, the widely read modern astronomer Carl Sagan sounds just like him. Sagan's *Pale Blue Dot* discourse includes this passage:

The Earth is a very small stage in a vast cosmic arena. Think of the rivers of blood spilled by all those generals and emperors so that, in glory and triumph, they could become the momentary masters of a fraction of a dot....Our posturings, our imagined self-importance, the delusion that we have some privileged position in the Universe, are challenged by this point of pale light. Our planet is a lonely speck in the great enveloping cosmic dark.

The modern science of Sagan and the Ptolemaic science of Boethius both provided the foundation for expressing very similar ideas. They came from extrapolating from what we can see, to what we imagine must lie beyond what we can see. And, as far as we know today, they seem to be right. Certainly, as astronomers have been able to see farther and farther in space (and back in time), there's nothing to suggest that this isn't the case.

But there's one aspect to this extrapolation that is no longer assumed. Aristotle's ideas and Ptolemy's mathematics provided what seemed like a solid foundation upon which to erect various ideas about the universe. A common feature of most cosmologies before the scientific revolution, including those based on Aristotle or Ptolemy, was the idea that the physical universe reflected the nonphysical, spiritual realm. This often involved positing a "chain of creation" in which different levels or aspects of the physical universe were assigned to different elements, different gods, or different ranks of angels.

By the middle ages, it was assumed that the home of the saints and the biblical firmament—the "dome" of Genesis— were the outer spheres of the universe; our tiny Earth stood not at the center of the universe but at the bottom of it—at the drain of the universe, or the sump of the universe, the place where the heavy elements like earth and water settled. It was, in the choice words of the Renaissance philosopher Giovanni Pico della Mirandola, the place of all the universe's "excrementary and filthy parts."[1] And since any dirt in the universe would naturally settle into the sump, into the lowest place, there would be only one Earth.

In the chain of creation, the surface of the Earth was still at least one level removed from the Inferno. Anyone with eyes could see fire and brimstone bubbling up through the giant holes in the ground in places like the island of Vulcano off Sicily. And, of course, Dante eventually described multiple layers of the Inferno beneath the Earth. For us, it's sufficient to emphasize that the "central" position of Earth in this cosmology did

---

1. See Pico della Mirandola, *Oration on the Dignity of Man*, http://www.history guide.org/intellect/pico.html.

not mean it was the most important place in creation. Rather the opposite since the Inferno is even more central than Earth!

Between the firmament and the Earth were the spheres of each planet, all made of that unchanging fifth element, the quintessence. Their perfect eternal circular motions, attributed to the varying ranks of angels, stood in contrast to the irregular and finite movements of objects on Earth.

In our modern view of cosmology, this picture has been completely abandoned. And yet it is worth appreciating how this Aristotelian cosmology was closer to the truth than the Babylonian (and biblical) picture of a flat Earth covered by a dome that had preceded it. Indeed, it was an essential step to bring us to where we are today: maybe not correct, not even almost correct, but more correct than what had come before— and correct enough to yield insights that have stood the test of time, as we see with Boethius and Sagan.

Nevertheless, theories built upon Aristotle's views began to be questioned well before the Scientific Revolution. Joannes Scotus Eriugena, writing the *Perphyseon, On the Division of Nature* in the ninth century, attempted to organize the understanding of creation on a theological basis. In discussing the natural world, Eriugena engaged in a long exegesis of Genesis and discussed what he had read in the Greek classics. Among other things, he wrote,

> The planets that revolve around the sun change their colors in accordance with the qualities of the regions they are traversing, I mean Jupiter and Mars, Venus and Mercury, which always pursue their orbits around the sun, as Plato teaches in the Timaeus.

Orbits around the sun! (Alas, it appears that he came up with this idea not out of some clever insight into the nature of the universe, though, but rather from misreading Plato.)

And he was not the first to have this idea: Martianus Capella, writing in Africa five centuries earlier, also spoke of the planets orbiting the sun, while the sun orbited a stationary Earth. And, of course, Aristarchus in ancient Greece had proposed a completely heliocentric system in the century after Aristotle.

When the Islamic university in Toledo, Spain, was captured by Christian forces in 1085, its library was translated into Latin. European universities received the knowledge of the Islamic world, including many works of Aristotle and Ptolemy that had been lost in the West, and newer Islamic commentaries on those works. But some people saw Aristotle's championing of an eternal universe, and his insistence that there is only one world (one Earth), as a challenge to the concept of an omnipotent Creator God. Disputes over the teaching of Aristotle broke out in Paris, attracting the attention of both the local bishop and the pope. In 1277, the bishop of Paris condemned the teaching of philosophers who believed that Aristotelian ideas were the ultimate authority of what was true.

These theological disputes gave philosophers, like Nicholas of Cusa—who was later made a cardinal in the church—and the great Jewish rabbi Maimonides, the incentive to look beyond Aristotle's cosmology. Cusa wrote a book called *On Learned Ignorance* (1440) in which he imagined every star as being a separate "world," and even thought about the difficulties of communicating with intelligent beings from those worlds.

But when it came to "almost correct," it's hard to beat Bishop Nicole Oresme, who in his *Book of Heaven and Earth* (1377) wrote,

> All motions are relative; if arrows fired eastward and westward had "natural circular motion" to the Earth's spin then one would not see any difference

in their flight. Reason alone cannot rule out the possibility of the Earth spinning and the stars holding still. Nevertheless, everyone holds that the heavens move and the Earth stands still; and so do I.[2]

John Buridan (d. 1358) also looked beyond the ideas of Aristotle to envision a different way of understanding the motions of the heavens. What if, he asked, there is more to the elements than just a natural resting place toward which they move? What if matter can be given a self-moving action—an *impetus*, he called it—dependent on an object's speed and the amount of matter in it? In that case, matter would then move just as naturally as it rests. He tested this idea with various experiments and used it to explain physical phenomena ranging from thrown stones to vibrating strings. He also envisioned a self-moving universe, put in motion at the beginning by God. Buridan's impetus anticipated the work of Isaac Newton and the modern concept of momentum. However, Buridan's ideas themselves were watered down, and corrupted by those who came after him, until his concept of impetus would merely be one of those ideas that was almost correct.

People like Eriugena and Buridan did not displace Ptolemy. Nicolas Copernicus would do that. In the early sixteenth century, Copernicus introduced the heliocentric theory, or rather, reintroduced it, since Aristarchus had developed it some two thousand years earlier. But there were serious scientific and philosophical objections to a heliocentric system— the same issues that were part of why it did not catch on with Aristarchus.

Indeed, there is a surprising amount of "science gone wrong" in the story of heliocentrism. No, we are not talking here about the whole refusing-to-look-through-the-telescope,

---

2. This is a very loose translation of Oresme's Latin.

science-denying, Bible-thumping stereotype of people refus-
ing to believe Copernicus. In fact, there was a lot less of *that*
going on at the time than you might think. Remember, Augustine accepted Ptolemy's ideas about the moon not being a
"great light" versus the stars, and simply interpreted the Bible
as describing things as they appear to our eyes. St. Thomas
Aquinas, and even John Calvin, said the same thing. (Calvin was
particularly enthusiastic about what astronomy revealed—
"this art unfolds the admirable wisdom of God," he wrote in
his commentary on Genesis 1:14–16.) If the science was persuasive, then people would come around.

"Persuasive"—there was the rub! Those serious scientific
and philosophical objections to heliocentrism were persuasive. In the generation after Copernicus, the Danish astronomer Tycho Brahe (d. 1601) latched on to a particularly difficult
problem with heliocentrism, one that St. Augustine would
have recognized: the sizes of stars. Copernicus realized that
if the Earth moved, while the sun and stars stood still, then by
looking carefully at the stars in the sky, you ought to be able to
see their apparent positions, one from another, shift back and
forth as the Earth moved around the sun. But no one had ever
seen such a motion. That required the stars to be much farther
away than even Ptolemy had placed them.

Ptolemy had said that the *Earth* was a tiny speck within
the universe; Copernicus said the *Earth's orbit* was a tiny speck
within the universe. That made the stars all that much farther
away—and all that much larger, for them to appear the size
they do in the night sky.

Brahe tried to figure out how far away, and how large,
the stars were. How could anyone measure that? Well, here
on Earth, one way is to see how big an object appears to us.
If you see two cars out in the distance, and one looks much,
much smaller than the other, then odds are it's farther away.

Of course, cars come in various sizes, but that range is small compared to the range of distances that they might be from us.

Brahe was obsessed with measuring the heavens. He built large, precise instruments that made it possible to make accurate measurements with just his naked eye. These instruments were something like giant protractors—the telescope had not yet been invented when he was observing—and with modern measurements, we can see just how good he was. And while a typical bright star in the sky might be small, nevertheless he thought he could measure how wide it was.

Brahe estimated that you might be able to fit ten to twenty bright stars across the disk of the moon. Since the moon, in turn, can almost exactly cover the sun during an eclipse, this meant that the typical bright star was about one-twentieth the width of the sun as well. So, if the stars were the size of the sun, they would have to be twenty times further from Earth than the sun. But if the stars were that close, then surely, he'd see the positions of the brighter (and hence closer) stars shift compared to the positions of the fainter (hence further) stars as the Earth moved annually around the sun...just as nearby trees seem to shift their positions compared to distant trees when you move about in the forest.

Brahe looked carefully for this effect, called *annual parallax*, and did not see it. So, he concluded that the Earth was not moving.

Of course, there was another possibility. Brahe recognized that this could also mean that the stars were just much farther away—too far to show any annual parallax. That is what Copernicus had said. But then they would also be much larger than our sun. By his calculation, to be seen as they are from Earth, the stars would not be just as large or larger than the sun, like St. Augustine had noted; the stars would have to be as large, or larger, than *Earth's orbit around* the sun. To Brahe, this enormity was unreasonable.

Fig. 1B. A star in an Earth-centered universe compared to a star in the sun-centered universe of Copernicus. The arrowed sphere indicates the size of the sun. The small sphere to its right is the size a typical star seen in the night sky would have to be in an Earth-centered universe to look as large as it does to our eyes. The large sphere is roughly the size that star would have to be in Copernicus's universe. This is because, in Copernicus's universe, stars had to be much more distant; and therefore, to appear as they do to our eyes, they had to be much larger.

Those who favored the Copernican system, though, would invoke God's power to explain this away. *Who is to say that a powerful God could not make giant stars?* they argued. *Perhaps stars are God's warriors, guarding the gates of heaven!*

Brahe himself, much like Capella and Eriugena, preferred the idea that the planets (note that he didn't think of the Earth as a planet) orbited the sun while the sun orbited a stationary Earth. He said this system was consistent with Aristotle's physics and with Scripture; and what's more, it didn't need those huge stars. Simon Marius (d. 1625), Galileo's rival in Germany, put the telescope to work supporting Brahe. The sizes of the stars that he measured in his telescope were smaller than Brahe had estimated, but still too big to be so far away without being giants.

But Brahe's assistant, Johannes Kepler, embraced the idea of giant stars: giant, and dim. After all, if all the stars in the nighttime sky covered an area of the sky comparable to that of the moon, why was it that their combined light was nowhere near as bright as the moon—much less the sun? And so, Kepler concluded that the sun was the unique, central, brilliant object in the universe. The giant stars and the small but brilliant sun showed God's ability to create on a vast scale, and yet pour care into even the smaller things of creation.

Kepler waxed poetic here. The stars were huge, yes, but the stellar part of the universe was inert, unmoving, and dull. The planetary realm was livelier, even if smaller. But it, too, was unchanging. "What it does (when moved)," he wrote in his 1604 book, *On the New Star*, "it did not learn, but it retains what was impressed upon it from the beginning. What it is not, it will never be. What it is was not made by it—the same thing endures that was created." Then Kepler looked at the Earth, so full of life. And on Earth, he said,

> Behold if you will the little bodies that we call the animals. What, in comparison to the universe, can be imagined that is smaller than these? But there now behold feeling, and voluntary motions—an infinite architecture of bodies.
>
> Behold if you will, among those [animals], these fine bits of dust, which are called human beings; to whom the Creator has granted such, that in a certain way they may beget themselves, clothe themselves, arm themselves, teach themselves infinite arts, and daily work toward the better; in whom is the image of God; who are, in a certain way, lords of the whole bulk.
>
> And who among us would choose a body the breadth of the universe in exchange for no soul? Let us learn, therefore, what well pleases the Creator, who is the author of both coarse bulks and minute

perfections. For he glories not in bulk, but ennobles those that he willed to be small.

Thus, Kepler envisioned that, while the Earth was not the central location in the universe, Earth's sun was, and we on Earth were of value in the eyes of God.

Kepler used this idea, which would have seemed to be on very solid ground at the time, to attack the ideas of Giordano Bruno. In the late sixteenth century, Bruno, who was enthusiastic about Copernicus's ideas, had proposed that the stars were other suns, orbited by other Earths in an infinite universe where we would have no significant place. Kepler, the astronomer, insisted that Bruno's ideas were refuted by basic observations. The stars were not other suns; they were much too big and much too dim.

> In case you're wondering...where did Brahe and Kepler and Marius all go wrong in their science? The answer is that the little disk of light that you see when you look at a star through a telescope, or with your naked eye, if your eyes are really good, is a sort of illusion. It's impossible to focus light to a perfect point because of the wave nature of light, something none of them could have known at the time. Instead, eyes and telescopes show stars as being slightly fuzzy dots, much larger than they should be. The light of the stars is spread across those dots, diminishing the intensity of the stars' brilliance. Brahe, Kepler, and Marius were seeing those fuzzy dots and interpreting them as the actual disks of the stars. Astronomers would not figure this out until much, much later.

The best science of the time may have supported Kepler's views, but Bruno's ideas captured the imagination. The stars being other suns was such an appealing thought! From the seventeenth century's Bernard Fontenelle, who argued for a "plurality of worlds" like Earth, through the nineteenth century's Mark Twain, whose Captain Stormfield found himself lost in a universe so populated with intelligent life that no one he met had ever heard of the Earth, to the twenty-first century's "Marvel Cinematic Universe" movies that teem with intelligent life and other worlds...it's wonderful to imagine that not only is the Earth a planet and the sun a star, but that we occupy a universe full of other suns with their own Earths, where we could find new life, new civilizations, and have new adventures.

But this idea, too, is changing. And it's worth considering how this change has occurred.

Kepler was right when he thought that, based on the science of his (and Bruno's) time, the stars could not be suns. But by the end of the seventeenth century, astronomers were slowly coming to understand that the apparent sizes of stars that astronomers measured might be erroneously large. (It took a long time for this realization to sink in; reputable astronomers like Jacques Cassini still talked about vast star sizes well into the eighteenth century.) In fact, there was almost nothing about stars that could be measured at all, and so this allowed people to dream of them as being, as Bruno said, other suns orbited by other Earths. It wasn't until the middle of the nineteenth century that telescopes, and our understanding of how light waves behaved, improved to the point where something about the distances and natures of stars could truly be determined.

Agnes Mary Clerke was a late-nineteenth-century multilingual Catholic one-woman hub for astronomical communication and knowledge. In her book *A Popular History of Astronomy during the Nineteenth Century*, she described what was known about the stars at her century's start, and what had been learned about them by its end. At the start, she wrote, very little was known; astronomers largely viewed the stars as a background against which the motions of planets were measured. Astronomers operated on the assumption that one star was much the same as another (and the same as the sun), so those stars that appeared faint to us must be more distant, and those that appeared bright to us, less distant.

That assumption turned out to be—you guessed it!—wrong. By the end of the century, Clerke wrote, the distances to roughly one hundred stars had been measured. Moreover, the list of stars with measured distances was "an instructive one, in its omissions no less than in its contents. It includes stars of many degrees of brightness, from Sirius down to a nameless telescopic star in the Great Bear." Many of the brightest stars had been found to be too far away for their distances to be measured, while most of the stars that were found to be nearest to Earth were quite faint. And so, she wrote,

> The obvious conclusions follow that the range of variety in the sidereal system is enormously greater than had been supposed, and that estimates of distance based upon [brightness seen from Earth] must be wholly futile. Thus, the splendid Canopus, Betelgeux, and Rigel can be inferred, from their indefinite remoteness, to exceed our sun thousands of times in size and lustre; while many inconspicuous objects, which prove to be in our relative vicinity, must be notably his inferiors. The limits of real stellar [brightness] are then set very widely apart.

In other words, there is a great diversity in size and brightness among stars. (Recalling the analogy we used above, different stars are far more varied in size than different cars.) And in the century and a quarter since Clerke wrote, the diversity of the universe has become more and more apparent. The sun may be a star; but very few stars are like the sun. Most stars are smaller than our sun; but some of them really are as big as the Earth's orbit around the sun!

To use Clerke's example, consider the hundred stars currently known to be the sun's nearest neighbors in space. About eighty of those have less than one one-hundredth of the sun's power output. All these eighty combined would not equal the sun. Most of the sun's nearest neighbors are not even visible to the naked eye.

What is more, of the thousands of planetary systems discovered around other stars so far, none of them is like our solar system. None. Likewise, we have yet to find a planet that is truly like the Earth, despite the breathless news releases issued regularly from various university astronomy departments.

Just a few decades ago, we thought that all planetary systems would be like our solar system. Circling our sun, there are the "terrestrial" planets of Mercury, Venus, Earth, and Mars; of these—Venus and Earth—both of similar size, are the largest. Then there are the "giant" planets of Jupiter, Saturn, Uranus, and Neptune; of these, Uranus and Neptune—both of similar size—are the smallest. There is a vast jump in size from Venus–Earth to Uranus–Neptune. And there was a time when we astronomers had a beautiful theory for why that jump existed and why, in fact, there *could not be* planets of size between Venus–Earth and Uranus–Neptune, anywhere. Except...we have discovered that, among those planetary systems orbiting around other stars, something like *half* the planets we see in the universe have sizes that lie in the "impossible" range between Venus–Earth and Uranus–Neptune! Talk about science gone wrong!

Our science swung from Aristotle's idea of there being just one Earth, to Bruno's and Marvel's idea of myriad Earths. Our expectations in this regard keep going wide of the mark. Even Johannes Kepler had imagined that Jupiter would be inhabited, but we have long known that Jupiter is a ball of gas without even a surface to stand on. Meanwhile, Venus is the size of Earth, but it is hotter than an oven, thanks to its atmosphere. Venus is utterly unlike Jupiter, and both are so unlike Earth as to be uninhabitable. And this goes on for all the planets in our own solar system. Our discovery of planetary systems around other stars has revealed planets of sizes that do not even exist in our solar system—types we once thought simply could not exist. And, unlike what we see illustrated in our favorite science fiction movies, in fact none of them really come close to being similar to Earth.

This tremendous diversity leads us again to think of our place in the universe. The Earth is indeed a planet, circling along with other planets, like Venus and Jupiter, around the sun, which is indeed a star. We can say this with a great deal of confidence.

But Earth is a particular kind of planet. The sun is a particular kind of star. Its planetary system is a particular kind of system. (And what have we yet to learn about our specific galaxy?) Our science is changing, and the more we learn the more we realize that we occupy a very particular place in the universe. "Behold if you will...these fine bits of dust, which are called human beings, to whom the Creator has granted so much."

Or so it seems now. Remember, what we know today isn't the last word. Today's right answer may turn into tomorrow's science gone wrong.

From this history, then, let's take three important lessons. First, each seemingly false step along the way was quite reasonable. The flat Earth covered by a dome, as described by the Babylonians (and seen in Genesis 1) is precisely what anyone can see simply by walking outside and looking around. That was just an extrapolation from what people could see with their own eyes. Likewise, the "four elements" of Aristotle were a reasonable idea, and echoes of them are found in our modern descriptions of the states of matter as solid, liquid, gas, and plasma. The geometrical constructions of Ptolemy, Brahe, and Kepler were each able to do a passable (and ever-improving) job of predicting where the planets might be seen in the sky on any given date. If all you needed was to predict where you could find the planets in the sky, they all were able to do that... at least over the times when human beings were able to look and record what they saw. Their ideas about the stars made sense and were quite reasonable given the knowledge of the time. They were all, in their own way, almost correct.

Second, note that each cosmology was born out of an imagined way that the universe *ought* to be, and in turn, fed the human imagination about our place in the universe. The medieval Christian adaptation of Aristotle provided the framework not only for the theology of St. Thomas but also for the literature of Dante and Chaucer. As such, it was adopted as much for the sake of its beauty and elegance as for any judgement of which system best fit the data. As C. S. Lewis points out in his book *The Discarded Image*, "Few constructions of the imagination seem to me to have combined splendour, sobriety, and coherence in the same degree."

But Lewis then notes the third key point to remember. "It is possible that some readers have long been itching to remind me that it had a serious defect: it was not true." All these cosmologies had value, but none of them were truth in itself.

Nor should we think our own cosmology, be it as seen in scientific or pop culture, is the finished story. (If we did come to such an ending, we'd have no more science to do, no more stories to invent...which would be a shame!) That grade school picture we mentioned at the start of this chapter might not be such a Right Answer after all, not because it is "wrong" but because it is woefully incomplete.

And in realizing this, we should honestly appreciate the achievement of each of the cosmologies that came before our own. The image of God as Creator who acts in an orderly fashion and loves every step of that creation, is as valid and important today as ever—even if the Earth is not the center (no, bottom) of the universe. Likewise, Dante is still worth reading. And our favorite science fiction stories remain a remarkable, and obviously appealing, example of our human capacity for imaginative storytelling—even if sun-like stars and Earth-like planets are not so typical in the real universe as they are in the Marvel one.

But every step on this journey, from the light-strewn dome to the thousands of (strange) exoplanets, also required a difficult choice at some point of realizing, and admitting, that what we had believed up to now was not good enough. It meant recognizing the point where our extrapolations were no longer valid.

It's hard to give up an image that has centuries of validation (or even just decades of validation), is intrinsically beautiful, and serves as a basis for the way we understand our place in the universe. It's hard to give up an idea that we thought had extracted deeper principles from the things that we see and had helped us to understand why things happen the way they do.

And it's especially hard to give it up for a new alternative that may itself turn out to be wrong after all!

Chapter 2

Copernicus and the High Seas

Recall the cosmology of Aristotle that we discussed in the previous chapter, with the four elements that made up the Earth, at rest at the center of the universe. The way the philosophers of the Middle Ages interpreted it, at the outer reaches of the universe was the firmament, the location of God. The Earth, at the center—at the bottom, really—was very distant from God (and beneath the surface of the Earth, at the very center and the farthest from God, the Inferno). Between the firmament and the Earth were the spheres of each planet, in perfect eternal circular motions, reflecting the varying ranks of angels. All part of the "chain of creation."

That's the broad picture, and it is well-known. But there was also a not-so-well-known, smaller-scale picture of the structure of our world. It was a remarkable, fascinating, and even enchanting theory, one that resulted from the words of the Bible being thoroughly mashed up with the ideas of Aristotle. It was the "Two Spheres Theory." This theory was a description of our world that may seem bizarre to our ears, and yet, still echoes in some common phrases in the language we use to describe how we experience life on Earth.

It was also science gone wrong...on a scale as big as the Earth itself.

The Two Spheres Theory arose from biblical passages that spoke of God gathering the waters into one place and letting the dry land appear; from certain obvious observations about the world's oceans; and from the Aristotelean idea of the four elements (earth, water, air, fire) that each had their own natural place. This strange view was, nonetheless, almost correct—it worked to explain what people saw and meshed with what they knew about the universe. But it worked for all the wrong reasons. Furthermore, it prevented anyone from thinking about a rotating Earth until a sailor from Genoa named Columbus accidentally provided the proof that this strange Aristotle-Bible mashup was in fact wrong, unwittingly spawning a revolution in science.

Aristotle's cosmology was a way of explaining the world around us. It involved what we might call laws of nature. Of course, we can explain the world without laws like that. Let's explain the rising and setting of the sun without laws of nature, for example. The Greek myth of Helios does that: *The sun is the glowing chariot of a god, Helios. Helios hitches up the horses every morning and rides that chariot across the dome of the sky. His daily ride is the cause of the rising and setting of the sun.*

In cultures throughout the world, unseen supernatural powers—gods, spirits, sprites, and other entities—are what make the world work. Of course, relying on gods to make the world work has an uncomfortable aspect to it. What if Helios gets tired of riding his chariot across the sky seven days a week, fifty-two weeks a year? If that happens, the sun may not rise tomorrow. The Earth will grow cold. Crops will die. Humanity will starve to extinction in the freezing dark.

If the world is run on the actions of gods like Helios, then we had better make sure that those gods have what they need so that they will happily keep on doing what we need them to be doing—like making the sun rise and set. This idea can get bloody. Human beings have been offered in sacrifice to make sure that the sun will rise tomorrow.

While the idea that the world is controlled by supernatural powers seems to be what people naturally gravitate toward, Aristotle's ideas suggest something entirely different. His ideas suggest that the world functions according to certain rules that are inherent in nature. No direct action by the gods or other supernatural entities like spirits or demons is required.

For example, imagine you have a large steel bolt and a piece of paper. You hold them out in front of you and release them both at the same moment. The bolt falls directly and rapidly to the ground. The paper flutters and floats its way down, reaching the ground significantly later than the bolt. Why did this happen?

An explanation based on the view that nature is governed by supernatural urges might say something about some affinity that the bolt or paper has for the Earth. The bolt is made of metal, material that was mined from the ground, heated, forged, and hammered into shape. By this way of thinking, the bolt was torn out of Mother Earth, and it yearns to return. The paper, by contrast, is made from plants. That material left the ground of its own accord. When released, it only reluctantly returns to the ground. Bolt and paper are each a mini-Helios, doing in part that which they want to do.

The language of this way of thinking remains today: sometimes people will say that loose objects in a moving car will fall backward and forward as the car accelerates and brakes because the objects "want" to remain in their state of motion; or that electric current "wants" to take the path of least resistance; or that a coin that has been tossed four times and has come up heads all four times is "due" to come up tails. This view suggests the possibility of magic. With the right gestures and words, we might convince the bolt that it does *not* want to fall, or the current that it does *not* want to take that path, and thus we might gain some control over at least a part of nature.

What Aristotle says, by contrast, is that the fall of the bolt and the paper is the result of certain rules inherent in nature. There are no direct actions of the gods, no "wants" of falling objects, involved. Each of the four elements that make up our world has a natural place in the universe toward which it will move. The natural place of the element earth is the lowest spot in the universe. Water also tends down to low places, but not so strongly as earth. Air has no tendency downward.

We can verify these tendencies easily. We fill a bottle one-third full of sand, one-third full of water, and one-third full of air; shake it to mix the three, then let the bottle sit. The sand (earth) will move to the bottom, followed by the water next; the air will be on top. The final element, not in our bottle, is fire, which tends upward toward the sky. It would rise upward through the air like the sand settles downward through the water. Thus, water and earth have "gravity," or heaviness. Fire has "levity," or lightness (Aristotle would probably view the helium we put in balloons as refined elemental fire). Air is in the middle.

The bolt, being material that was mined from the ground, heated, forged, and hammered into shape, is nothing but refined earth. You cannot get it to release water, air, or fire. Hold a match to it and nothing happens. Being earth, it there-fore has a very strong tendency to move down. Release it, and down it goes. It does not go down because it "wants" to go down; it goes down for the same reason that it is solid, that it is rigid and holds its shape—that is the nature of the "earth" element.

What is the paper made of? Among other things, wood—trees. Trees grow in earthy soil, true, but trees also require water, air, and warmth and light. Wood is not pure. It is a combination of elements. Paper, which is made from wood, is also a combination of elements. When it burns, we see fire being released from it. The paper will naturally not move toward the ground as readily as the bolt.

In Aristotle's ideas, there are no gods moving things, no objects wanting to go this way or that. The bolt and the paper fall because of what they are made of, and because of some basic rules of nature—rules of "gravity" and "levity." There is not so much room for magic here. We may not recognize Aristotle's theories as correct science today, but they were scientific; they were much closer to correct than what came before them.

Aristotle's ideas suggest a larger structure to the universe. Fire should move up, until it is stopped by something else—the "fifth element" not found on Earth, which makes up the heavens and has a natural tendency to move in circles. The moon is the heavenly body closest to earth, so the fifth element must start at least there. So, under the moon, high above us, and surrounding the earth we stand on, should be a sphere of fire. Under the fire, then, should be a sphere of air, also surrounding the earth. Under the air, a sphere of water. And at the center should be a sphere of earth—what we stand on. Just like the bottle experiment. (That's how you know science is correct, right? When you have an experiment to show how things work!)

We stand on the sphere of earth. We are immersed in the air. The fire sphere would be far above; maybe it's the red glow in the sky we see at sunset, or in the aurora borealis.

So where is the water?

Indeed, various people argued that, in fact, there should be progressively more fire than air, more air than water, and more water than earth—maybe ten times more by volume in each case. Were this the case, the earthy sphere on which we stand should be wholly submerged.

WHEN SCIENCE GOES WRONG

The Two Spheres Theory answered the "where is the water" question. The theory said that the sphere of earth was *partially* enveloped by a larger sphere of water; but in fact, the earthy sphere bulged out from the watery sphere. The earthy bulge included the entire dry terrestrial world known to the Jewish, Christian, and Islamic thinkers who so closely studied the ideas of Aristotle: Europe, Africa, and Asia. The center of the terrestrial bulge was typically taken as being Jerusalem. Jerusalem is more than thirty degrees north of the equator (about the same latitude as Savannah, Georgia, or Shanghai, China). So, if we look at the world aligned north-south, it would be a sphere of water with an off-axis earthy bulge sticking out about a third of the distance from the equator to the north pole—or, if you prefer, a sphere of earth partly covered by a watery sphere that's been pulled out, opposite Jerusalem, about a third of the way from the equator to the south pole.

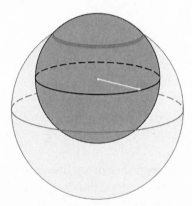

Fig. 2A. In the "Two Spheres Theory," our world consists of a sphere of earth (darker in this illustration) that is partially enveloped by a larger sphere of water. The earthy sphere bulges out from the watery sphere, and that bulge comprises the terrestrial world. The earthy sphere would not be smooth as in this simple diagram, but rather quite rough, since the dry land has high mountains and deep valleys. Where those irregularities exist along the edge of the ocean (the water sphere), they would beget coastal islands even as large as Britain, and inlets even as large as the Mediterranean Sea.

But how could this be? Why doesn't the water cover the earth? Why aren't the earthy sphere and the watery sphere arrayed around the same center, the way that Aristotle suggested they ought to be?

There were a couple of ways by which this could be explained. One idea was that the earthy sphere has cavities within it, and thus is buoyed up by the water sphere: the earth is floating in the water! The other explanation was that the water had been displaced from its natural position, and so the water sphere had a center other than the center of the universe, that is, the center of gravity. This meant that on one side of the world, water stood higher than the land. Ships sailing out to sea would then be sailing "uphill": *the high seas*. And as they sailed out, the ocean would get deeper, and deeper—tens, hundreds, even thousands of miles of watery depths beneath the keel of a ship: ♫*I'll tell you a tale of the bottomless blue....*♫

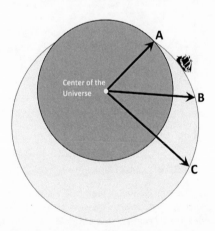

Fig. 2B. If the earthy sphere lies at the center (bottom) of the universe, and the watery sphere is displaced from its natural position, then a ship that leaves a port at A and heads out to sea moves away from the center of the universe. It sails "uphill" as it moves to B and then C. The water stands higher than the land. At B and C, the depth of the water might be hundreds of miles or more.

WHEN SCIENCE GOES WRONG

This idea is so strange that it is worth repeating for clarity. This idea was that (1) the center of the earthy sphere was the center of the universe, that is, the lowest place in the universe and the center of gravity; (2) the watery sphere was off-center to the earthy sphere; and from (1) and (2), it then follows that (3) some points on the watery sphere would be farther from the center of the universe—that is, higher—than dry land. The ocean would be higher than the land and unfathomably deep.

Fig. 2C. Illustration by Gaspar Schott of Jean Bodin's idea that the Two Spheres Theory could explain springs. Water passing through channels within the earthy sphere comes up through the ground, Bodin had said, in the same manner that water comes up though leaks in the bottom of a ship. Schott notes that the water sphere (on the bottom, marked by A, B, C) would be much larger than is shown here.

This helps to explain a natural phenomenon—water springs! Especially big water springs! And extra especially big springs in the middle of the desert or up on the side of a mountain. What could feed a big spring that supplies a desert oasis? There is no rain. Instead, there must be cracks in the earthy sphere that allow water from the ocean to work its way through—water that is under pressure and rises up from the ground owing to the fact that the ocean is higher than the land and water seeks its own level. In 1663, the German Jesuit Gaspar Schott in his book *The Physical-Hydrostatic Anatomy of Springs and Rivers* shows illustrations of this phenomenon.

This idea that the seas were higher than the land was in fact taken as common knowledge. For instance, in the 1688 book *Familiar Letters, Domestic and Forren*, by James Howell, we can find a letter of April 1, 1617, from James to his brother, in which he writes,

> I am newly landed at Amsterdam, and it is the first forren Earth I ever set Foot upon....He that observes the site and position of this Country, will never hereafter doubt the truth of that Philosophical Problem which keeps so great a noise in the Schools, viz. That the Sea is higher than the Earth; because, as I sailed along these Coasts, I visibly found it true; for the Ground here, which is all 'twixt Marsh and Moorish, lies not onely level, but to the apparent sight of the Eye, far lower than the Sea; which made the Duke of Alva say, That the Inhabitants of this Country were the nearest Neighbours to Hell of any People upon Earth, because they dwell lowest.

Once you spend enough time thinking about this idea, you can almost begin to convince yourself that it makes some sort of sense. For example, there are times when you can stand at the shore of the ocean and see that the sea horizon is, in fact, slightly higher than you expect. The English astronomer Richard A. Proctor described this in an article he wrote for the September 7, 1883, issue of *Knowledge: An Illustrated Magazine of Science, Plainly Worded, Exactly Described*:

> Nearly every one must have noticed that when you are in an inland road near the sea, at a considerable height above the sea-level, you are apt when you get a sudden view of the sea-horizon to find it much higher than you had expected. This is particularly the case if there are steep side-tracks leading down towards the sea from the road you are following and if you have had reason to note the steepness and depth of these side-tracks as you advance, without however seeing the sea itself for some time. Then when you come upon an opening leading to the sea, you look *down* for the sea-horizon and find that you must turn your eyes upwards to see it: not upwards in reality, nay in reality somewhat though not perceptibly downward, but upwards from the direction in which you had first looked expecting to see the horizon.

Granting, then, that the sea does appear to stand higher than the land, we ask, How can this be? Doesn't water seek its own level? Why don't the waters of the ocean flow over the land? What could keep the oceans higher than the lands so that their waters feed the springs? The obvious answer to someone who was steeped in both Aristotelean physics and biblical cosmology was, "the hand of God."

There are several verses in the Bible that could be read as endorsing this idea—that say that it is God that holds the seas back (all these are King James Version—it's appropriate to the time in question):

> And God said, Let the waters under the heaven be gathered together unto one place, and let the dry *land* appear: and it was so. (Genesis 1:9)

> In the six hundredth year of Noah's life, in the second month, the seventeenth day of the month, the same day were all the fountains of the great deep broken up, and the windows of heaven were opened. And the rain was upon the earth forty days and forty nights....And the waters prevailed exceedingly upon the earth; and all the high hills, that *were* under the whole heaven, were covered. Fifteen cubits upward did the waters prevail; and the mountains were covered. (Genesis 7:11–12, 19–20)

> By the word of the LORD were the heavens made;
> and all the host of them by the breath of his mouth.
> He gathereth the waters of the sea together as an
>   heap:
> he layeth up the depth in storehouses.
>   (Psalm 33:6–7)

> *Who* laid the foundations of the earth,
> *that* it should not be removed for ever.
> Thou coveredst it with the deep as *with* a garment:
> the waters stood above the mountains.
> At thy rebuke they fled;
> at the voice of thy thunder they hasted away.
> They go up by the mountains;
> they go down by the valleys unto the place
> which thou hast founded for them.

WHEN SCIENCE GOES WRONG

Thou hast set a bound that they may not pass over;
that they turn not again to cover the earth.

(Psalm 104:5–9)

When he prepared the heavens, I [Wisdom] *was*
there:
when he set a compass upon the face of the depth:

When he established the clouds above:
when he strengthened the fountains of the deep:

When he gave to the sea his decree,
that the waters should not pass his commandment:
when he appointed the foundations of the earth:

Then I was by him, *as* one brought up *with him.*

(Proverbs 8:27–30)

Clearly the Bible shows that the nature of water is such that it will cover earth, just like both Aristotle's theory of elements and our bottle experiment say. And just as clearly, the Bible tells us that the fact that the water does not cover the earth is a sign of God's mighty action. What or who else on Earth could be more powerful than the sea? Yet it is held back.

And from this we find the strangest product of this mashing up of religion and science—the seas being thought of as proof of the existence of God! In his mid-sixteenth-century lectures on Genesis, Martin Luther said that "it is most true that the sea is much higher than the earth," so today God's power and presence are displayed as clearly as at the Red Sea's parting. Then there is this, from *A Sermon against Atheism: Preach'd at the Parish-Church of St. Martin in the Fields, Novemb. 24. 1700* by Tho. Knaggs:

The Bounds and Limits which are set to the Sea, which by a perpetual Decree it cannot pass, may let us see the Finger of God is there. *Hitherto shalt thou go and no further*, proclaims a God. God himself asks *Job* this Question, *Who hath shut up the Sea with Gates, when it brake forth as if it had issued out of the Womb?* [Job 31:8] That the Sea is higher than the Earth, is what Men of sound Reason lay down for a certain Truth, and consequently would overflow the Land, was it not stay'd by an Almighty Hand, that will not permit that raging Element to go beyond its appointed Bounds, and makes it recoil back again, even when it threatens the Shore with its terrible Waves and Roars.

There was a time when the Earth was covered with the Deep as with a Garment, and had not the Providence of God broke up for it his decreed Place, it had still continued such a Garment to the Earth, as the Skirt that was made for the Murthering of *Agamemnon*, where the Head had no place to get out. *I brake up for it my decreed place; I set bars and doors, and said hitherto shalt thou come, but no further: And here shall thy proud waves be stay'd*, said God [Job 31:10–11]. *They that go down to the Sea in ships, and do business in that raging Element: These Men see the Works of the Lord, and his Wonders in the Deep* [Ps 107:23–24].

The language of Knaggs conveys his awed respect and fear for an ocean that is so deep that no cable could possibly sound its depths, and that would easily swallow up the earth but for the will of God.

In 1673, Thomas Vincent's *An Explicatory Catechism: Or, an Explanation of the Assemblies Shorter Catechism* discusses the same thing, but more briefly:

Q7. What is the first Argument to prove that there is a God?

A. The first Argument, to prove that there is a God, may be drawn from the Being of all things [including 1. The Heavens, 2. The Earth and] 3. The Being of the vast Sea, where there is such abundance of Waters, as some think, higher than the Earth, which yet are bounded and refrained from overflowing and drowning the Land and its Inhabitants, as once they did when their Limits were for a while removed....

Vincent's *Catechism* was reprinted for over a century—in 1701, 1720, 1777, and 1806.

Clearly, using an idea with its roots in the Two Spheres Theory to argue for the existence of God did not work out so well in the long run. Science changes. It goes wrong. It is not what you want to base your theology on.

One of the people behind the demise of the Two Spheres Theory was a scientist: Copernicus. The other, however, was an explorer: Christopher Columbus!

As every school child knows, Columbus had the radical idea that one could reach the spice traders of India and China by sailing west around the world from Spain. The radical part of his idea was not that the world was round; that had been well established since before the time of Aristotle. Indeed, two centuries before Christ, Eratosthenes in Egypt had, in fact, determined the circumference of this round world by measuring and comparing the length of shadows cast by the sun at noon on the same day but at different latitudes. If that measurement was correct (and, spoiler alert, it was), then it meant that the Earth was so large that no ship available at the time of Columbus could have carried enough supplies to make it all the way around to India. They would have run out of food and fresh water before they got halfway there.

Columbus compared these ancient measurements and argued that, in fact, Asia was much closer...thanks to several errors that he committed, all of which served to improve his chances. He confused the size of the "mile" used by the Arabs, who had preserved and reported the ancient Greek work, with the Italian "mile," which was considerably shorter. And he assumed an exaggerated size for Asia (based on the stories of Marco Polo), which meant he wouldn't have to travel so far to reach it by crossing the opposite sea.

But notice what also went without saying in Columbus's calculation. He also assumed that, of course, there couldn't possibly be any other land mass between Spain and Asia. Why? Because the Two Spheres Theory meant that all the land in the world was concentrated on one side of the world, and Spain was at the western edge of that land mass.

Copernicus's book, *On the Revolutions of Heavenly Spheres*, came out in 1543, fifty years after Columbus's notable voyage. By that time, of course, it was clear that there was indeed a "new world" across the Atlantic that was very different from Asia. Copernicus's book is famous for its proposition that our world is a planet circling the sun. It is less known for its discussion on the structure of the Earth, a discussion that attacks the Two Spheres Theory.

Within book 1 of *On the Revolutions*, Copernicus includes two chapters discussing the shape of our world. Chapter 2 of book 1 he titles "The Earth Too Is Spherical." He writes,

> The earth also is spherical, since it presses upon its center from every direction. Yet it is not immediately recognized as a perfect sphere on account of the great height of the mountains and depth of the valleys....For a traveler going from any place toward

39

the north, that pole of the daily rotation gradually climbs higher, while the opposite pole drops down an equal amount. More stars in the north are seen not to set, while in the south certain stars are no longer seen to rise. Thus Italy does not see [the star] Canopus, which is visible in Egypt. (Copernicus wrote in Latin—this is an English translation.)

This observation of how the stars change as we move northward or southward is a standard argument for why we know the Earth is round; it is the star-based equivalent of Eratosthenes's sun-and-shadow observations. Then, a little further on, Copernicus continues:

The waters press down into the same [spherical] figure also, as sailors are aware, since land which is not seen from a ship is visible from the top of its mast. On the other hand, if a light is attached to the top of the mast, as the ship draws away from land, those who remain ashore see the light drop down gradually until it finally disappears, as though setting. Water, furthermore, being fluid by nature, manifestly always seeks the same lower levels as earth and pushes up from the shore no higher than its rise permits. Hence whatever land emerges out of the ocean is admittedly that much higher.

Note how Copernicus discusses water separately from "earth," showing that water is likewise round. It seems that what Copernicus means by "the earth" is actually just "the dirt and rock stuff" or "the earthy stuff."

Following the discussion of the water comes chapter 3, entitled "How the Earth Forms a Single Sphere with Water." This reads as follows:

Pouring forth its seas everywhere, then, the ocean envelops the earth and fills its deeper chasms. Both [earth and water] tend toward the same center because of their heaviness. Accordingly there had to be less water than land, to avoid having the water engulf the entire earth and to have the water recede from some portions of the land and from the many islands lying here and there, for the preservation of living creatures. For what are the inhabited countries and the mainland itself but an island larger than the others?

This seems like a straightforward description of our world if you are not aware of the Two Spheres Theory. But Copernicus was aware of it. And so, the next thing Copernicus does is to address that very idea:

We should not heed certain peripatetics [Aristotle enthusiasts] who declared that the entire body of water is ten times greater [in volume] than all the land....They also assert that the earth bulges out to some extent as it does because it is not of equal weight everywhere on account of its cavities, its center of gravity being different from its center of magnitude.

That the Two Spheres Theory is wrong, Copernicus says, can be established

by the fact that from the ocean inward the curvature of the land does not mount steadily in a continuous rise. If it did, it would keep the sea water out completely and in no way permit the inland seas and such vast gulfs to intrude.

41

Of course, a devotee of the theory could counter that the earthy sphere is obviously no perfect sphere—it has those high mountains and deep valleys that Copernicus mentioned earlier. Deep valleys in the earthy sphere at the point where it meets the watery sphere would allow for inlets, and even for the entire Mediterranean Sea—the sea in the *middle* of the terrestrial region.

But Copernicus continues, also noting that, were the theory correct,

> the depth of the [oceanic] abyss would never stop increasing from the shore of the ocean outward, so that no island or reef or any form of land would be encountered by sailors on the longer voyages.

In other words, if the Two Spheres Theory were correct, then as a ship sailed out from land into the ocean, the water would only get deeper and deeper. Because of local irregularities of the same nature as valleys and mountains, one might expect to find some islands not too far from the shoreline, but no land masses should be found once a ship had been out to sea for a while. There should be no land on the opposite side of the world.

And yet, says Copernicus, new lands have been discovered in addition to the lands known to the ancients. These include

> the islands discovered in our time under the rulers of Spain and Portugal, and especially America....On account of its still undisclosed size it is thought to be a second group of inhabited countries....Indeed, geometrical reasoning about the location of America compels us to believe that it is diametrically opposite the Ganges district of India.

The existence of the Americas—discovered just fifty years prior to the publication of *On the Revolutions*—demonstrates that the Two Spheres Theory *cannot* be correct. Copernicus concludes that our world must be the sort of body that we today know it to be:

> From all these facts, finally, I think it is clear that land and water together press upon a single center of gravity...that, since earth is heavier, its gaps are filled with water; and that consequently there is little water in comparison with land, even though more water perhaps appears on the surface. The earth together with its surrounding waters must in fact have such a shape as its shadow reveals, for it eclipses the moon with the arc of a perfect circle...it is perfectly round, as the philosophers hold.

In 2015, historian David Wootton argued in his book *The Invention of Science* that the discovery of America, which provided Copernicus with a solid argument by which to reject the Two Spheres Theory, was crucial to the development of his idea that Earth circles the sun. The Earth in the heliocentric theory must rotate about that north-south axis that we mentioned earlier to explain the rising and setting of the sun, moon, and stars. It is hard to imagine how a world that is a ball of water with an earthy bulge, centered on Jerusalem, bobbing out an angle, could ever rotate. A ball of rock, however, with a little bit of water on its surface, could. And if the Earth could rotate, then the universe could be heliocentric. The voyage of Christopher Columbus was crucial for the Copernican Revolution and the dawn of modern science.

But what about everyone thinking that the seas obviously stood higher than the land? The explanation for that probably lies not in water or earth but in air.

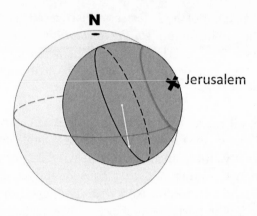

Fig. 2D. If Earth circles the sun, then it must rotate about its north and south poles so as to account for the rising and setting of the sun. A ball of water with an earthy bulge, centered on Jerusalem, bobbing out an angle, would seem unlikely to rotate in this manner.

Air refracts—bends—light rays. Everyone sees this on summer days, when heated air rising from hot surfaces like parking lots or roof tops makes distant objects seem to shimmer and waver. Those who have spent time at the eyepieces of telescopes know the effect that the air has on telescopic views; for example, the refraction caused by turbulent air on nights of "poor seeing" can greatly reduce the amount of detail that is visible on the planets. Furthermore, refraction by the atmosphere not only causes the sun and moon to have an oval appearance when rising and setting, but it causes the stars to rise earlier and set later than they otherwise would.

All this has been long known. In 1614, Johann Georg Locher wrote (also in Latin, of course) a brief discussion of refraction, especially regarding the sun, for his book *Mathematical Disquisitions*. He wrote the book with his teacher, Fr. Christoph Scheiner, SJ (the same Scheiner whom Galileo would later quarrel with over sunspots). Here is their discussion:

The elliptical shape of the sun is nothing other than a contraction of the solar globe in height, especially noticeable at the horizon, even to the unaided eye. Over time, ignorance of this phenomenon has given birth to, nourished, and maintained many errors in regard to astronomy and optics—errors which the acquisition of knowledge will take away. The elliptical sun is spawned by a perpendicular refraction that also explains many other things: why the sun appears higher than it should be; why the days are longer than they should be; why the relative positions of stars at the horizon are distorted; why stars linger at the horizon when rising or setting; and other phenomena.

Note the "linger at the horizon" comment. If we look out to sea to watch a star set and focus on a star above the Earth's equator—like the uppermost star in the belt of Orion, Mintaka—we find that the star seems to slow as it approaches the horizon. At the equator, where the setting of a star is straight down into the water, the delay is more than two minutes. In other words, if we watch stars wheeling overhead and measure their speed, and extrapolate to when they should set, we find that they set more than two minutes later than expected. The air bends Mintaka's light around the curvature of the Earth, holding it up in view when geometrically it is below the horizon. And as the atmosphere raises up Mintaka into view, it must be raising up miles of water into view also—the water seen just below the setting Mintaka.

How much water? Well, the Earth's circumference measures 25,000 miles, and the Earth rotates once every twenty-four hours. Thus, the speed of the Earth's surface at the equator is 25,000 miles / 24 hours, or over 1,000 miles an hour. That's over fifteen miles per minute. With over two minutes of delay in Mintaka's setting, that translates into something like forty to fifty miles. Thus, thanks to atmospheric refraction, when we see Mintaka set at the equator, we are seeing it set as it would be seen forty or fifty miles to the west, were there no atmosphere.

Geometrically speaking, we should only be able to see maybe a few miles out over the ocean. The air brings miles and miles of water up into view, water that ought not be visible; the sea really does look as though miles and miles of it rise into view, so that to sail out to sea might be to sail "uphill." The idea of the "high seas" may seem pretty crazy to us today, but if people did not understand the atmospheric refraction, then it might have been logical for them to conclude that the seas were "high," just as people like Howell and Knaggs said. They were, indeed, almost correct!

(This effect should also be true looking across land as well, of course. But it is unlikely to be noticed since even a low hill or line of trees will block the view to the distant horizon.)

It would seem, then, that the Two Spheres Theory grew out of both the ideas of Aristotle and basic observations of what the sea looks like, all reinforced by the words of the Bible. It actually makes some sense once you start looking at it. But it was science gone wrong. Before Copernicus's heliocentric theory could work, this wrong science had to go away. Yet, recall the 1806 edition of Vincent's *Catechism*; it still persisted in some circles, as part of discussions on religion, for another 250 years after Copernicus!

Let's pause here and consider further just how this wrong science called the Two Spheres Theory arose. On the one hand, people had an ever-growing sense of the size and shape of the world, mostly covered with oceans. They had Aristotle's kind of commonsense physics that noted that water typically sits on top of land, not the other way around. But then they had biblical sources that, at least in the translations in common use at the time, could be easily interpreted to explain both how water could be kept from covering over the land and indeed *who* would have been responsible for doing it.

The trouble goes beyond the obvious fact that this Two Spheres Theory twisted the meaning, and the translation and intent, of Scripture (much like tying Scripture up with the sizes of the moon and stars, as we saw in the previous chapter). The deeper problem was in the very intent of those who wanted to mash Scripture and science together.

This kind of mashup has a name: "concordism." Concordism has been a temptation for as long as clever folks have wanted to conform their familiar interpretations of Scripture with their naïve faith in science. You find concordism most alive today in those who try to mash together the idea of the Big Bang with the statement at the beginning of Genesis, "Let there be light!" The Big Bang says the universe began in a burst of energy, right? And light is energy, right?

But that mashup doesn't work for several reasons. First, it gets harder and harder to make the days of Genesis match up with the evolution of geology and life on Earth; the science doesn't work. But more importantly, identifying the Big Bang with creation misses a point known long before the theory of the Big Bang (you can find it in St. Thomas Aquinas): the creation *ex nihilo* by God is not just one event at a particular time, say 13.7 billion years ago. It is, in fact, the creation of space and time itself. That means that God's creation occurs equally at all times, and all places. And its truth does not depend on any specific understanding of how (or even if) there was a Big Bang.

Yet even a pope can mashup Scripture and the Big Bang. In 1951, Pope Pius XII, who had a keen interest in science (and in the Vatican Observatory), gave an address on "proofs for the existence of God in light of modern natural science." Speaking of the Big Bang theory, which had been proposed by the Belgian physicist and priest Fr. George Lemaître just two decades earlier, Pope Pius said that science "has succeeded in being a witness to that primordial 'Fiat Lux' [let there be light], when, out of nothing, there burst forth with matter a sea of light and radiation." Fr. Lemaître, understanding that sometimes science goes wrong—even the science he himself developed—spoke to the pope to convince him to avoid that concordism. (And Pope Pius XII subsequently did later avoid promoting that argument.)

But Pius XII was in good company. Who else went the concordist route? Galileo! In 1615, he wrote a famous letter to Christina of Lorraine, who was both mother of the then grand duke of Tuscany (Galileo's patron) and occasionally Tuscany's de facto ruler. In 1613, Christina had challenged Galileo's ideas—not his discoveries, mind you, but his support for the heliocentric system. She was worried about heliocentrism's apparent conflict with Scripture (recall from the last chapter Tycho Brahe and the scientific arguments against heliocentrism at the time).

Galileo gave Christina a concordist argument that Scripture actually agreed better with heliocentrism. He argued that the rotation of the sun (that he helped discover, by watching sunspots move across the face of the sun) powered the whole solar system, so that if the sun stopped, the whole system would grind to a halt, as though sun, moon, and planets were all connected by some invisible gear train. *Therefore*, he went on, when Joshua prayed for the sun to "stand still" and extend the daylight (Joshua 10:12–13), what God *really* did was to make the sun's *rotation* "stand still." This then halted the whole solar system, including Earth's rotation—the gears all ground to a halt, extending the day! And *furthermore*, Galileo said, for various reasons all this fit with Scripture *much better* than the idea that the Earth was at rest and God stopped the sun from circling it.

It was all a ludicrous mashup of science and Scripture.

Today the Two Spheres Theory looks as ludicrous to us as Galileo's gear train idea; and it is, for many obvious reasons. But the Two Spheres Theory has one last "almost correct" aspect to it, akin to Aryabhata's getting the age of the Earth right (for all the wrong reasons), and as fun as Joshua and the invisible solar system gear train.

While sea level is indeed level, and pretty much the same all over the world, there is in fact a slight difference between the levels of the Atlantic and Pacific Oceans, due to several factors such as their slightly different salt contents. The level of the Pacific is higher than that of the Atlantic (by just a little bit—roughly a foot). And it is the case that the Pacific Ocean can mostly be fit into one hemisphere of the Earth, while the opposite hemisphere contains most of the Earth's dry land (along with the Atlantic and a few other seas). If you do a mathematical mapping of all the dry land on Earth, including the Americas, depending on the assumptions you make, you can find that the geometrical "center" of that dry hemisphere is located anywhere between Egypt and Bulgaria...not all that far from Jerusalem!

Chapter 3

The Earth Does Not Spin

Politicians are notorious for "spinning" the news to fit their agendas or their self-interest. But they aren't the only ones guilty of making the facts fit the way they want the world to look. Scientists are only human. And in fact, one of the strengths of science is its ability to interpret the world through the perspective of an overarching cosmology. The more different aspects of reality that you can explain with one worldview, the stronger your faith in that way of understanding the world. Therefore, what could be more natural than looking at some fuzzy result and declaring that it confirms what you already knew to be correct?

That temptation to spin reality—something we call "confirmation bias" (we are biased in favor of evidence that confirms what we believed already)—was never more evident than in the discussions among early modern astronomers on whether or not the Earth itself was spinning.

If the Earth we stand on is a rocky world, then it might be able to spin about itself like Copernicus (and Aryabhata) proposed. That rotation would make the sun, moon, and stars

50

appear to rise and set daily. But just because the Earth conceivably *could* spin did not mean that it, in fact, *did* spin. And, in the decades after Copernicus published his 1543 book *On the Revolutions*, the question of whether the Earth was spinning or not was a matter of importance to many people—a matter that led to some remarkable, and almost correct, scientific ideas.

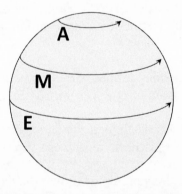

Fig. 3A. If the Earth spins daily around its axis, then the surface of the Earth (and everything on the surface) moves, and the speed of movement changes with latitude. At the equator (E), the speed is over 1000 mph, because points on the equator are traversing the full circle of Earth's 25,000-mile circumference in 24 hours. At mid-latitudes (M) the circle is smaller, and in the arctic (A) the circle is smaller still. Thus, the speed of Earth's surface is greatest at the equator and decreases to zero at the poles.

The idea of Earth spinning would matter to people because, for one thing, Earth's immobility seems to be a matter of common sense. If Earth does spin, then at this very moment you are moving very fast...indeed, frighteningly fast. Recall from the last chapter that the circumference of the Earth at its equator is about 25,000 miles, and Earth would have to turn completely around in twenty-four hours. That means that at the equator, Earth's rotation would translate into the ground moving at more than one thousand miles per hour! Yikes!

WHEN SCIENCE GOES WRONG

True, that speed drops to zero at the poles. But even at latitudes as high as the Arctic and Antarctic circles the spin of Earth implies ground speeds of hundreds of miles per hour. Do you feel like you are traveling, right now, at a speed far faster than the top speed of the fastest sports car?

Earth's spin would also matter because of that "concordism" mentioned in the previous chapter. It was obvious that the Bible suggests that Earth does not move at all, and the sun rises and sets by virtue of its own motion, all in agreement with Aristotle's science:

> *Who* laid the foundations of the Earth, *that* it should not be removed forever. (Psalm 104:5, KJV)

> The sun also ariseth, and the sun goeth down, and hasteth to his place where he arose. (Ecclesiastes 1:5)

> Then spake Joshua to the LORD in the day when the LORD delivered up the Amorites before the children of Israel, and he said in the sight of Israel, Sun, stand thou still upon Gibeon; and thou, Moon, in the valley of Ajalon. And the sun stood still, and the moon stayed, until the people had avenged themselves upon their enemies. *Is* this not written in the book of Jasher? So the sun stood still in the midst of heaven, and hasted not to go down about a whole day. (Joshua 10:12–13—the verses that inspired Galileo to concordism himself.)

So it seems that a spinning Earth violated both common sense and Scripture. Did it really make sense to explain the rising and setting of the sun by supposing us all to be hurtling eastward at prodigious speeds that we have no sense of whatsoever? Was not the biblical idea of Earth as fixed beneath our feet not the simpler, more logical, more reasonable, more elegant idea, and one concordant with the ideas of Aristotle?

That is not to say that the Bible *proved* that Earth did not move. Recall from the first chapter our discussion of Augustine, Boethius, and the question of star sizes. St. Augustine did not say that just because Genesis 1:16 calls the sun and moon the "two great lights" in the firmament of the heaven that it necessarily follows that the stars are indeed smaller than them. He did not necessarily put Scripture over Ptolemy's science.

St. Thomas Aquinas took a similar view in the thirteenth century. In his *Summa Theologica*, question 70, discussing the fourth day of creation, he notes the objection that "as astronomers say, there are many stars larger than the moon. Therefore, the sun and the moon alone are not correctly described as *the two great lights*." To this he answers,

> As Chrysostom says, the two lights are called great, not so much with regard to their dimensions as to their influence and power. For though the stars be of greater bulk than the moon, yet the influence of the moon is more perceptible to the senses in this lower world. More over, as far as the senses are concerned, its apparent size is greater.

In other words, Aquinas, like Augustine, accepted the results of the astronomy of his time (still that of Ptolemy). He interpreted the Bible in light of those scientific results as describing the heavens as they appear to us. He specifically rejected what we're calling concordism.

The same approach could be taken regarding Earth's motion. Those biblical verses that speak of Earth as fixed and the sun as moving could be interpreted as describing things as they appear to us. Even if Earth rotates, the sun does rise

WHEN SCIENCE GOES WRONG

in the east and the sun does go down in the west, and when it rises again, it is in the east, like Ecclesiastes says.

But the rule was that you did not do this lightly. You took the Bible's words in their plain sense whenever possible. In 1612, as Galileo was discovering many new things with his telescopes and advocating for Copernicus's ideas, he asked the opinion of Cardinal Carlo Conti about Scripture and Copernicanism. Conti replied, in a letter of July 7, that Scripture did not oppose new discoveries such as sunspots, which went against Aristotle's idea that the heavens were unchanging, but he noted,

> Where Scripture says that the sun revolves and the heavens move, it cannot have any other interpretation [outside of the literal interpretation], except that it speaks in conformity with the common mode of the average person; this mode of interpreting must not be admitted without great necessity.

Cardinal Robert Bellarmine would tell Galileo pretty much the same thing, in a letter of April 12, 1615:

> If there were a true demonstration that the sun is at the center of the world and...does not circle the Earth but the Earth circles the sun, then one would have to proceed with great care in explaining the Scriptures that appear contrary, and say rather that we do not understand them than that what is demonstrated is false. But I will not believe that there is such a demonstration, until it is shown me...and in case of doubt one must not abandon the Holy Scripture as interpreted by the Holy Fathers.

So, you don't abandon the plain sense of the Bible, the sense that the church fathers read, unless necessary—unless there is no doubt that the plain sense does not hold up, as with the "great lights" in Genesis (and as with other places in the Bible, such as Malachi 1:3, where God, who is love, comments, "I hated Esau [Jacob's brother]"). Was it *necessary*, then, to abandon the plain sense of the Bible's description of a fixed Earth and a moving sun? For all that has been said regarding science versus religion in the Copernican Revolution, ultimately the question was just a matter of science.

There were scientific arguments in favor of the idea that we could all be hurtling eastward at a prodigious speed and have no sense of that motion whatsoever. Those who supported Copernicus said that if everything was moving together, the motion would be undetectable. Galileo, in his 1632 *Dialogue Concerning the Two Chief World Systems: Ptolemaic and Copernican*, would nicely explain this Copernican "common motion" position by imagining the cabin of a ship:

> Shut yourself up with some friend in the main cabin below decks on some large ship, and have with you there some flies, butterflies, and other small flying animals. Have a large bowl of water with some fish in it; hang up a bottle that empties drop by drop into a narrow-mouthed vessel beneath it.
>
> With the ship standing still, observe carefully how the little animals fly with equal speed to all sides of the cabin. The fish swim indifferently in all directions; the drops fall into the vessel beneath; and, in throwing something to your friend, you need throw it no more strongly in one direction than another, the distances being equal; jumping with your feet together, you pass equal spaces in every direction.
>
> When you have observed all these things carefully (though there is no doubt that when the ship is standing still everything must happen in this way),

have the ship proceed with any speed you like, so long as the motion is uniform and not fluctuating this way and that.

You will discover not the least change in all the effects named, nor could you tell from any of them whether the ship was moving or standing still. In jumping, you will pass on the floor the same spaces as before, nor will you make larger jumps toward the stern than toward the prow even though the ship is moving quite rapidly, despite the fact that during the time that you are in the air the floor under you will be going in a direction opposite to your jump.

In throwing something to your companion, you will need no more force to get it to him whether he is in the direction of the bow or the stern, with yourself situated opposite. The droplets will fall as before into the vessel beneath without dropping toward the stern, although while the drops are in the air the ship runs many spans. The fish in their water will swim toward the front of their bowl with no more effort than toward the back, and will go with equal ease to bait placed anywhere around the edges of the bowl.

Finally the butterflies and flies will continue their flights indifferently toward every side, nor will it ever happen that they are concentrated toward the stern, as if tired out from keeping up with the course of the ship, from which they will have been separated during long intervals by keeping themselves in the air. And if smoke is made by burning some incense, it will be seen going up in the form of a little cloud, remaining still and moving no more toward one side than the other.

> The cause of all these correspondences of
> effects is the fact that the ship's motion is common
> to all the things contained in it, and to the air also.

Indeed, experiments like this on a ship in constant, straight-ahead motion will not reveal whether the ship is moving or not, for exactly the reasons Galileo describes.

But the Earth is not a ship moving along with such motion. It turns, so Galileo and the Copernicans insisted; it turns on its axis. And indeed, everything that Galileo said about motion on a ship becomes completely wrong once the ship starts turning. If Galileo had actually spent any significant time on an oceangoing sailing vessel, he would have seen that everything down below has to be tied down securely to prevent it from flying about in the cabin during the voyage—not only due to the waves, but also during the sudden turns that a ship makes when it tacks into the wind.

Just recall how you feel pushed against the passenger-side door of a car when your driver makes a sudden left turn (or right turn, in Britain). In fact, it's the car being twisted into the path you used to be traveling in, so that the door pushes you sideways even as your momentum tends to keep you going straight forward. Shouldn't we be able to notice something like this being-forced-sideways effect, if we're riding on the surface of a rotating (turning) Earth?

Those who argued against Copernicus seem to have understood this better than Galileo. Tycho Brahe was one. The Danish astronomer lived from 1546 to 1601, just between when Nicolaus Copernicus published his theory that Earth orbits the sun, in 1543, and when Galileo started his telescopic observations, in 1609. Brahe admired many aspects of Copernicus's ideas, but he did not accept them, for several reasons, as we discussed in chapter 1.

One of these reasons was that Copernicus required that daily or *diurnal* rotation of the Earth about its own axis. Brahe recognized that a rotating Earth implied a difference in motion between the poles and the equator as we illustrated in Figure 3A (page 51): objects at the equator being carried along by Earth's supposed rotation at over one thousand miles per hour; objects at the poles hardly moving at all. Everything on Earth did not, in fact, share a common motion like objects in the cabin of a ship. Brahe felt that this difference should produce observable effects. In his 1601 book *Astronomical Letters*, he wrote that "near the poles of the Earth, where the diurnal motion (if such might exist) comes to rest" a ball fired from a cannon should be expected to travel in the same manner regardless of which way the cannon is aimed. Yet, "in the middle between each pole at the Equator, where the motion of the circumference of the Earth ought to be fastest," the situation should be different.

Brahe was no physicist. He did not discuss what exactly he expected to be different between poles and equator. He just said that "since these [cannon shots] may come about uniformly everywhere, indeed it is necessary that Earth rest uniformly everywhere." After all, if Earth is immobile, then every place on its surface is equally immobile. Simple. Elegant.

Brahe developed his own ideas about the working of the universe. He supposed the Earth to be indeed immobile, and circled by the sun, moon, and stars. The planets, however, circled the sun. So far as the apparent motions of anything in the solar system are concerned, this arrangement is identical to that of Copernicus; nothing you could see in a telescope like Galileo's of the sun, moon, and planets could tell the two arrangements apart. As Johannes Kepler said, "In Brahe the Earth occupies at any time the same place that Copernicus gives it, if not in the very vast and measureless region of the fixed stars, at least in the system of the planetary world." Brahe's system was as compatible with the new telescopic discoveries as was the system of Copernicus.

Brahe's system offered the advantages of the Copernican system and got around certain disadvantages. There was no need to explain those cannonball trajectories discussed above. There was also no need to explain how a great, heavy ball of rock and water—the "hulking, lazy Earth," as Brahe put it—could be made to move. Recall that the physics of Aristotle assumed celestial bodies like the sun were made of the "fifth element," material different from the Earth, that moved naturally; Newtonian physics was far in the future.

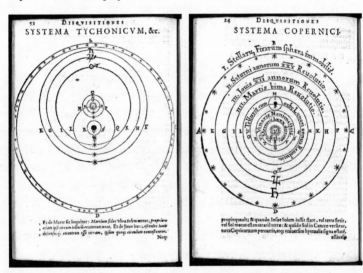

Fig. 3B. Tycho Brahe's theory about the working of the universe (left) compared to that of Copernicus. Brahe supposed the Earth to be immobile, and circled by the sun, moon, and stars (with the planets circling the sun). These two systems gave identical results regarding any observations of the sun, moon, or planets made from Earth's surface. Nothing a telescope of the time could show could tell these two arrangements apart. These diagrams are from the 1614 book *Mathematical Disquisitions*, by Fr. Christoph Scheiner, SJ, and his student Johann Georg Locher.

Public domain images courtesy of E-rara, the portal for digitized printed works from Swiss libraries.

And there was no need to explain biblical passages that described the sun as moving and the Earth as fixed. This was an issue in the sixteenth century, despite what Augustine and Aquinas had said in earlier centuries. The Protestant reformers had complained that the unreformed church was too lax in how it interpreted the words of the Bible. John Calvin, who agreed with Augustine and Aquinas in accepting that astronomy showed stars to be larger than the moon, and who praised astronomy as a "pleasant" and "useful" art that "unfolds the admirable wisdom of God," nevertheless described those who "will say that the sun does not move, and that it is the earth which shifts and turns" as "deranged" and possessed by the devil. Thus Brahe, living in the Protestant north, described his system as one that "offended neither the principles of physics nor Holy Scripture."

A decade after Brahe, another astronomer, Fr. Christoph Scheiner of the Society of Jesus (whom we met in the last chapter), endorsed Brahe's system as the most elegant and most consistent with observations. In doing so, however, he said Brahe had appropriated it from the ancient African writer Martianus Capella; the fact that Brahe was a Protestant while Scheiner was a Catholic may have led him to temper his praise of Brahe. In his 1614 book *Mathematical Disquisitions*, Scheiner and his student Johann George Locher also noted the issues that a rotating Earth raised regarding objects moving above its surface at differing latitudes.

However, they focused on objects rising and falling, rather than on projectiles like cannon balls. Starting with the premise that "everyone, even Copernicans, acknowledges heavy bodies to be pulled down toward the center of the Earth along a vertical line," Locher and Scheiner asked their readers to consider three identical balls carried around with the rotating Earth, high above its surface: one above the equator, another above a mid-latitude point, and a third above a pole.

When these balls are let fall, they ask, how is it that the ball falling at the equator would follow a path that is basically a flat spiral, the ball at mid-latitudes would follow a conical spiral, and the ball at the pole would fall straight down? And what about the differing speeds that result from different heights above the Earth's surface?

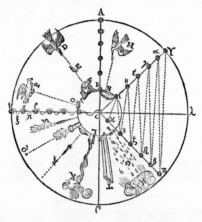

Fig. 3C. Illustration by Locher and Fr. Scheiner of how falling objects on a rotating Earth must move if people everywhere on Earth's surface see falling objects as travelling straight down. The axis of rotation is horizontal. Ball V falls at the pole. There the surface of the Earth has no speed; the ball just falls straight toward the Earth. Ball A falls at the equator. There the speed of Earth's surface is greatest; the ball's motion is Earthward and forward, in a spiral. Ball Y falls at mid-latitudes. It has a triple motion along a conical path.

Public domain image courtesy of E-rara, the portal for digitized printed works from Swiss libraries.

Unlike Brahe, Scheiner and Locher were not concerned about how the "hulking" Earth could move. They had developed an explanation for Earth's orbit, saying that it might be like the fall of an iron ball attached to a bent pole stuck in the ground. When the pole topples over, the ball moves in a circular path. (Not much science gone wrong here; many decades later Isaac Newton would explain an orbit in terms of his theory of gravity and a perpetual fall, and that is still how we describe orbits today.) They were also not hung up on concordism. They were willing to grant that words in Scripture about the "rising and setting" of the sun might actually describe the horizon "setting and rising" (convoluted as that may seem, they noted).

Still, they concluded that the questions they raised argued against any motion of the Earth. "Innumerable absurdities arise" because of that motion regarding "all things moving up or down," they said, and so "therefore the motion of Earth need not be granted." Brahe, Locher, and Scheiner could see no observable effect of the Earth's spin on either projectiles or falling bodies at different latitudes. To them, this lack of evidence served as an argument for Earth's immobility. It was not necessary to set aside the plain sense of the Bible.

Mathematical Disquisitions made a big impression on Galileo. He devoted many pages of his *Dialogue* to casting *Disquisitions* in a negative light. He made jokes in the *Dialogue* about the figure reproduced here.

And then he contested Scheiner and Locher's statement that everyone agrees that heavy bodies fall straight down to Earth. He wrote that if Earth rotates, then a ball held in a high place would be carried around by Earth's rotation in a larger circle than, and therefore move faster than, the ground to which it falls. So, when the ball is let fall, it should "run ahead" of the ground and be deflected eastward.

Elsewhere, Galileo argued for another effect caused by Earth's rotation: a cannonball launched toward a target located due east of the cannon should strike above its intended mark, he said, because the rotation of Earth carries the target downward while the ball is in flight (as the "horizon sets"); conversely, a ball launched west should strike below its mark. Galileo even worked out the magnitude of this effect: one inch of deflection for a ball that takes one second to travel from cannon to target. Since in fact such shots are typically off from their target by up to a yard, he said, this deflection is completely unobservable.

In 1651, Fr. Giovanni Battista Riccioli, also of the Society of Jesus, took the deflection idea further in his book *New Almagest* (unhumbly named after Ptolemy's great book, the *Almagest*). Like Galileo, he argued that on a rotating Earth, objects will not fall straight to the ground but will instead be deflected to the east. Then he discussed projectiles. This discussion shows some in-depth physical thinking that he attributes to his assistant, Francesco Maria Grimaldi, another Jesuit.

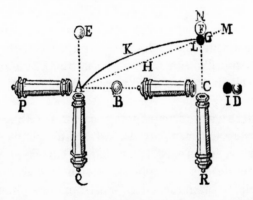

Fig. 3D. Fr. Riccioli's complex cannon illustration. The straight path AHL is what the ball launched northward would follow were the Earth like a ship, with all points moving together at the same speed. The curved path AKF is what the ball follows because the ground speed changes. It is very close to what modern calculations give for the path of a projectile moving over a rotating surface.

Image from the library of the Vatican Observatory.

Riccioli noted Brahe's argument about Earth's rotation and cannonballs flying at the poles and at the equator. He noted how the speed of the ground is faster toward the equator and slower toward the poles. And then he went on to discuss a heavy cannon being shot at a target located 250 paces to the north. Were the cannon aimed straight at the target, he said, the ball might hardly hit it, but would rather graze it. This is due to the ball's trajectory having been sufficiently distorted by the "strength of the diurnal motion" that the ball ran ahead (east) of the target. The ball was moving east faster than the target! And if another target were placed to the right, or east, of the first target, he said, the ball would plow straight into that second target, and carry it further to the right.

Riccioli provided a rather complicated illustration of this north-fired cannonball veering slightly eastward because of changing ground speed. Riccioli considered the absence of any such observable effect to be a key argument in favor of Earth's immobility. Riccioli agreed with Brahe's idea that the sun circles the immobile Earth, while planets circle the sun.

Brahe, Locher and Scheiner, and Riccioli were all building a powerful scientific argument that the Earth was indeed immobile. There was no need to reexamine traditional interpretations of the Bible.

And here we see science going wrong. Why? Because these scientists were, in fact, *almost* correct. The deflection effect they were describing does exist. It is called the *Coriolis effect.*

The hurricanes that spin into North America every summer and fall are dramatic, often catastrophic, manifestations of the Coriolis effect, which is very important in weather patterns. The effect is regularly discussed in modern textbooks and popular science books, and the discussion usually goes something like this, by astronomer and popular author Phil Plait:

> At the equator you are moving nearly 1,030 miles per hour to the east....At Sarasota, Florida...you are moving east at 930 mph....Now imagine someone on the equator due south of your [Sarasota] position takes a baseball and throws it directly north.... Relative to you, that baseball is moving 1,030 mph

– 930 mph = 100 mph or so to the east by the time it reaches you. Even though the fastball is aimed right at you, it will miss you by a pretty wide margin!

In the atmosphere, air drawn toward a low-pressure zone deflects (like this baseball) east if it approaches the zone from the equator; it deflects west if it approaches from the pole. This sets up a circulation around the "low." The circulation is counterclockwise in the northern hemisphere, clockwise in the southern. This is the source of a hurricane's rotation.

The Coriolis effect bears the name of Gaspard-Gustave de Coriolis. He worked out the detailed mathematics of the effect in the early nineteenth century. But obviously, the idea behind the effect was developed almost two centuries prior to Coriolis, largely by people such as Riccioli—*who did not believe that it existed*.

What about Galileo's argument that effects like these that were caused by a rotating Earth would be too small to detect? Here is another example of science gone wrong. Riccioli believed that the gunners of his time were so skilled that they could place a shot precisely into the mouth of an enemy's cannon. With that kind of precision, any difference in the trajectories of cannonballs fired in different directions certainly would have been noticed. The fact that they had not, indicated to him that Earth was immobile.

Riccioli was not alone in his ideas. Christopher Wren, the architect of St. Paul's Cathedral in London, once described gunners as knowing how to fire a cannon upward and make the ball drop right back into the mouth of their own cannon. In fact, Italian experimenters in the seventeenth century also claimed to have been able to fire a cannon vertically and have the ball fall right back to the cannon's mouth.

Why would anyone think that gunners could be so precise? Who knows? This idea was not correct at all, and in fact not everyone thought gunners were so accurate. The letters of Rene Descartes speak to the failures of experiments with cannons, where the ball might be launched upward and, rather than falling back into the mouth of the cannon, might never be found at all.

But mistaken ideas can endure in science. At least one mistaken idea about the accuracy of guns and the Coriolis effect endures to this day. An often-repeated story used to illustrate the Coriolis effect claims that, during the naval Battle of the Falkland Islands in December 1914, the British were surprised to find that they initially missed their German opponents by over one hundred yards. This was because, so the story goes, they did not account for the fact that, south of the equator, the Coriolis effect would operate in the opposite direction from what British gunners would have accounted for in the Northern Hemisphere. For over half a century, this story has been a regular feature in physics textbooks produced by prominent authors and publishers. And it's completely bogus!

For one thing, the British and Germans had fought other actions off Brazil and Chile earlier in that year, so the story that the British were surprised by something peculiar to the Southern Hemisphere does not ring true. Moreover, the effect of the Earth's rotation was minor compared to the difficulty of shooting at distant, moving targets from a rocking, moving platform at sea. Reports from the time, such as a book on the battle written during the war by Commander H. Spencer-Cooper with input from those who fought it, mention a variability of *two hundred yards* in a single volley of shots as being evidence of good gunnery. And it never mentions the Coriolis effect.

So where did this oft-cited Falklands story come from? Apparently, it was published originally in the 1950s by the mathematician John Edensor Littlewood, in a somewhat cryptical fashion, as an interesting-but-not-necessarily true anecdote. However, once it got into the physics literature, it was repeated for decades. It seemed to be an excellent and interesting example of the Coriolis effect.

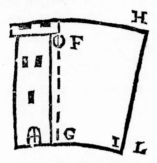

Fig. 3E. Simple illustration by Fr. Dechales showing how, were Earth rotating, a falling ball could not travel straight down. The Earth's supposed rotation carries the top of a tower eastward more rapidly than the bottom. A ball dropped from the top would share the motion of the top. Therefore, when released (at F), the ball would not fall to the bottom of the tower (at I) but would travel as far as the tower top did, hitting the ground away from the tower at L.

Image from the library of the Vatican Observatory.

Sometimes science goes wrong by repeating stories that don't hold up to scientific examination, but do appeal to scientists. Stories of accurate guns appealed to, and confirmed the biases of, scientists like Riccioli in the seventeenth century, and still do today.

Interestingly, even had gunners been as accurate as Riccioli imagined, they would have noticed no difference between shots sent toward the north or south versus those sent east or west. A full mathematical analysis of the Coriolis effect reveals that, at a given latitude, the effect is independent of direction. This is not intuitive; discussions of the effect usually treat only the intuitive examples of objects moving north or south, as in Plait's discussion above.

Though Riccioli worked out much of what we now call the Coriolis effect, Claude Francis Milliet Dechales in his book *Mathematical World* (published in 1674 and again in 1690), wrote an illustrated discussion of it that could have come from a textbook today. In a section entitled "Objections against Copernicus," Fr. Dechales (the fourth astronomer from the Society of Jesus in our story!) included an illustration of a tower carried by a rotating Earth and argued that a ball dropped from its top would not fall straight down, but would travel farther toward the east, because of the greater speed of the top of the tower versus the ground.

He also included an illustration of a cannon aimed at a target to the north. The diagram shows the cannon and the target both carried to the east by the Earth's rotation, but with the cannon carried farther east, and the ball that it fires at the target carried farther east as well, so that it misses the target to the right.

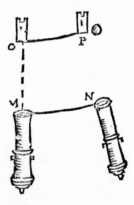

Fig. 3F. Simple illustration by Fr. Dechales showing how, were Earth rotating, a cannon fired northward could not shoot straight. Earth's supposed rotation would carry the cannon eastward more rapidly than its target; the ball it launches, which shares its motion, would deflect to the east (right), as seen at P.

Image from the library of the Vatican Observatory.

In his book, Dechales cites Riccioli. However, his qualitative treatment of these effects is more straightforward than

Riccioli's, and his diagrams are clearer. His discussion differs little from modern qualitative discussions of the Coriolis effect, like the one from Phil Plait above. We would call his discussion correct.

You will not be surprised, however, to hear that Dechales thought these deflections, which he explained so well...did not exist! Like Riccioli, he saw his derivations as being objections against Copernicus, arguments against Earth's rotation.

With sufficiently careful setups, the Coriolis effect can indeed be detected in projectiles. Long-distance target shooters have put some interesting Coriolis effect videos on the internet. However, the first easily visible demonstration of the Coriolis Effect involved not projectiles or falling bodies, but pendulums.

Remember that, in the Northern Hemisphere, the Coriolis effect causes a north-moving object to deflect eastward—to the right—and a south-moving object to deflect westward—also right. Now, imagine this occurring, not in a single large movement to the north or south, but in many small, repeated movements to the north and south, such as would occur in the case of a pendulum swinging in a north-south plane. Every northward swing yields a tiny rightward deflection. Every southward swing yields another tiny deflection, again rightward.

Each individual deflection is effectively negligible. But as the pendulum swings back and forth over the course of a day, these negligible deflections add up, and the plane of the pendulum's swing is altered. Because the Coriolis effect is independent of direction, the plane continually rotates. This was first demonstrated, in 1851, by Léon Foucault in Paris, two centuries after Riccioli's *New Almagest* first described the effect behind it. Foucault pendulums are commonly featured in science museums today as an illustration of Earth's rotation.

Fig. 3G. Foucault pendulum at the Kentucky Science Center in Louisville, Kentucky.

And while pendulums were revealing Earth's rotation, the motions of high- and low-pressure systems were becoming understood. Across the surface of the Earth, air motions are both large enough in scale and high enough in speed for the Coriolis effect to produce a dramatic effect in the atmosphere, but only in the nineteenth century were such weather patterns discovered. At that time, naval officers—notably Matthew Fontaine Maury of the U.S. Navy—collected the extensive records of weather patterns from navy vessels traversing the globe to correlate data about winds and currents. Meanwhile, the invention of the telegraph allowed meteorological offices in Europe to collect and correlate weather data at the same time on a continental scale, thus making evident the cyclonic patterns produced by the Coriolis effect.

But it fell to one more Jesuit in the early twentieth century to demonstrate the Coriolis effect with a slightly different approach—at the Vatican itself. Johann Georg Hagen was born in Austria in 1847. After being ordained a priest in 1878, he was sent to the United States, where he became an American citizen. He taught mathematics at Sacred Heart College at Prairie du Chien, Wisconsin. He built a small observatory there and began to study variable stars. Then, in 1888, he was appointed director of the Jesuits' Georgetown College Observatory in Washington, DC, where he published the first three volumes of his monumental atlas of variable stars, the *Atlas Stellarum Variabilium*. Finally, in 1906, Hagen was called back to Europe to become the first Jesuit director of the Vatican Observatory, then located on the walls surrounding St. Peter's in Rome.

Hagen was fascinated with finding proofs from mechanics for the Earth's rotation. He gathered and examined all of the attempts made up until that time to measure the Earth's rotation. Then he invented two experiments of his own.

The first was his "Isotomeografo," which he installed on the basement floor of one of the Observatory's telescope domes. A twenty-eight-foot horizontal beam was hung by a two-strand steel cord about twenty-three feet long. Two small lead carriages weighing about two hundred pounds each were driven along the beam on symmetrical tracks, from the middle toward the ends and back. As the carriages moved, the Coriolis effect would cause the beam to undergo a small but measurable rotation in the horizontal plane. This was only the second experiment to demonstrate that the Earth was spinning, after Foucault's famous pendulum.

Fig. 3H. Photograph of Fr. Hagen's "Isotomeografo" at the Vatican Observatory. Note the two wheeled carriages and the scale for measuring deflection of the apparatus.

Image from the library of the Vatican Observatory.

The second invention involved setting up a large Atwood machine in a seventy-five-foot-high stairwell at the Vatican Museum. An Atwood machine slows down a falling object by connecting it over a pulley to a counterweight; it allows for a careful study of the falling object's motion. By using a clever downward-looking telescope, Hagen was able to follow the path of a falling object, as the Earth spun underneath it, and measure the spin of the Earth to better than 1 percent accuracy. When these results were reported at the Fifth International Congress of Mathematicians in Cambridge, in 1912, Hagen received an enthusiastic ovation.

Thus, Fr. Hagen confirmed the intuition of Frs. Scheiner, Riccioli, Grimaldi, and Dechales—and refuted their conclusion about the spin of the Earth!

The Coriolis effect is not limited to the Earth alone. The effect merely requires extensive motions across a rotating surface to be visible. That can be any rotating surface. It turns out that different planets offer a unique way to see the importance of these different factors of motion and rotation.

Venus is a case in point. Thanks to intense solar heating, large convection cells—"Hadley Cells"—can develop to move hot air from the equator to the cooler zones near the poles on the nighttime side. The result of this efficient transport of heat is that the atmosphere of Venus is essentially the same temperature everywhere. But the spin of Venus is so slow that there is essentially no Coriolis effect, and thus no cyclonic systems in its atmosphere.

Fig. 31. The cyclone-free clouds of Venus (left) vs. the swirling clouds of Jupiter seen by the Juno mission (right).

NASA images.

By contrast, the spin rate of Jupiter is so fast, and Jupiter is so large that its atmosphere is being carried around at a rate that is extremely rapid, compared to Earth, and changing rapidly with latitude. This results in the complex patterns of storms and clouds, from the Great Red Spot to smaller cyclonic features, which the recent Juno mission has illustrated so well.

There is much irony in all the science gone wrong regarding the Coriolis effect. There is irony in how the effect was first described, in a manner suiting a modern textbook, by astronomers who did not think that it existed, and who thus took its apparent absence as evidence that Earth does not spin. There is a further irony in how both scientists in the past, who mocked the effect, and scientists more recently, who wanted a dramatic textbook example of it, latched on to stories that exaggerated how the effect could be seen in artillery projectiles. And there is the additional irony that the Vatican, which had become infamous for opposing Earth's motion, became the site of two independent, delicate experiments demonstrating that very motion by using various versions of the effect.

Then there is the final irony that the Coriolis effect, originally envisioned as something that would not exist anywhere and thus by its absence would be scientific evidence defending the immobility of Earth and Aristotle's physics of difference between the Earth and celestial bodies, is now seen to exist even on other planets, thus being scientific evidence for how the same physics applies both on Earth and on celestial bodies.

Notice, however, that this is a different sort of science-gone-wrong story from the previous chapters. The science behind the Coriolis effect that was being developed by Riccioli and others was not "almost correct." It *was* correct. In fact, it was excellent science, and indeed ahead of its time, given that it is taught today.

So how did it go wrong?

The problem was confirmation bias. The authors of the

science thought they already knew the answer they were looking for. They *knew* that the Earth couldn't possibly be spinning—to think something as big as the whole world could somehow be moving around itself violated all the physics they'd accepted since Aristotle, for nearly two thousand years. This discussion of the effects one could look for on a spinning Earth was not something they expected to see; to them, it was just a clever thought exercise to demonstrate the absurdity of the notion.

Modern popularizers are no better, of course (and since this book is about science for a popular audience, its authors are at least among those trying to be popularizers of science). Once we have learned about Coriolis effects, we start to think we can see them everywhere, from naval battles to flushing toilets! (Yes, there are lots of internet squabbles about whether the swirl of water going down the toilet is evidence for Earth's rotation.) It's hard to admit that this interesting effect is very subtle, and any number of other effects (the motion of a battleship, the direction of an inlet pipe) can overwhelm the tiny deflection effect we're expecting to see. That doesn't mean the effect isn't there, just that reality is often more complicated than we want to believe, leaving plenty of space to let our confirmation bias convince us otherwise, and making room for a great story about naval battles.

Today confirmation bias is a popular and potent idea. Have you heard the terms *extrapolation* or *concordism* in casual conversation or in the media during the past week? Probably not. But the chances that you have heard *confirmation bias* are greater, and the chances that you have heard *bias* with implicit reference to confirmation bias—meaning people are set on having their own ideas or worldviews confirmed—are greater still. The idea of bias is so strong today that it is common to hear that there is essentially no such thing as truth, and that we live in a post-truth society; I can speak "my truth," you can hold "your truth," but our biases (especially *yours*) will keep us (especially *you*) from finding *the Truth*.

Yet the actual attainability of truth is part of what makes this chapter's science-gone-wrong story different. People's biases did not prevent scientific discovery. Science has shown that Earth's rotation, which Scheiner and others were certain did not happen, *does* happen. It has shown that the Coriolis effects they thought did not exist, *do* exist. Those effects did not show up in the dramatic fashion of guns missing their marks over long ranges as enthusiasts imagined; too many other factors buried the effects there. No, they showed up in subtle things—boring things, even. The Earth's spin was revealed in a pendulum, whose swing changes over a span of hours, and in the deflections of the beam of Fr. Hagen's Isotomeografo and of his slowly descending weight in that Vatican stairwell.

The biases of human beings have no influence on whether or not the Earth spins. The laws of physics and mathematics (governing the movement of a tower, or a cannon on Earth's surface, and governing the path of a ball dropped from that tower or launched by that cannon) are not determined by how many human beings hold a certain worldview. This is God's world; we just live in it.

But we can discover the ways that God has caused the world to follow "laws that never shall be broken" (as the old hymn "Praise the Lord! Ye Heavens, Adore Him," paraphrases Psalm 148:6). God has determined that the world is orderly, and knowable through scientific investigation—so much so that Dechales could produce textbook-quality diagrams of the Coriolis effect in action when he had never observed the effect and believed it to not exist. (This is why we said in chapter 1 that Genesis is the book that makes science possible.) Once human beings started thinking about the idea of a spinning Earth, and how that spin might be detected, our biases were not going to prevent us from ultimately discovering the truth.

We understand this implicitly. One of the authors of this book, Chris Graney, taught astronomy to community college students in Kentucky for many years. Those students had often been deprived of any kind of good education. Some had no education beyond grade school. Some had no knowledge of science at all; they were unaware that stars were more distant than the moon, or had never heard of protons, neutrons, and electrons.

At the same time, they were often very aware of the idea of bias, and fully accepted the concept of a post-truth society. Bigfoot? Real. The Apollo moon landings? Faked. The government was hiding a lot. (Everything, really.) The system was rigged. It was biased...against *them*. Why, they asked (sometimes with words, sometimes with attitudes), should we believe scientists like *you*, Prof. Graney, who are certainly part of that system?

The answer was to ask them to look to the rising of the sun. It was best if the class could step outside and look around—a break in the expected routine of schooling that grabbed everyone's attention. Prof. Graney, the scientist, points and says that the sun will rise over *there*, in that direction we call "east." Then the professor says to imagine that someone else, maybe a very famous and influential person, says that no, the sun will rise *there*, in the direction we call "north." What is more, that person is so influential that he has pitched his idea to the entire country at great expense. The idea is all over the internet. Repeated polling has now shown that indeed 82 percent of the country agrees that the sun rises in the north.

The students always completely and immediately understood that the sunrise question would be settled by gathering before dawn and watching the sun rise. The students always understood what truth was. The only way to *not* discover it was to not go look. They knew that, when the sun came up, our biases would not matter. They also knew that it didn't matter how many people believed that the sun rose in the north, or how famous and powerful the advocates for a northern sunrise might be. The students understood something Fr. George V. Coyne, SJ (the long-time director of the Vatican Observatory under Pope John Paul II), once said regarding science: "The truth is not democratic! The truth is true or not regardless of how many...think it is true."

All scientists understand this, even the ones who think they are atheists and make loud proclamations to that effect. Of course, people of faith understand this, too. Science and faith are together in recognizing that the truth exists, independent of our own biases or those of the popular or powerful. And truth can be discovered, so long as we care to go out and look for it.

That process of discovery can go wrong, both in science and in faith. We can find ourselves certain that the Earth is immobile, and certain that we have worked out a great argument showing why we are right. In such a case, it's useful to have a community of others—other scientists, other churchgoers—whom we can trust to keep us honest, or at least on our toes. But so long as we are seeking to discover the truth, our biases will not stifle that discovery, not in the long run.

Chapter 4

Jupiter's Slippery Moons

Maybe you remember the scene from *Harry Potter and the Order of the Phoenix*. Harry's know-it-all friend, Hermione, is correcting his astronomy homework at Hogwarts, when she wryly informs him that his answers about the moons of Jupiter are *almost* correct: "Europa is covered in ice, not mice."

Br. Guy Consolmagno, SJ, half the writing team of this book, remembers that scene well. As soon as he read it, he thought to himself, "Hey! That's my master's thesis!"

Hogwarts is a work of the imagination, of course. It takes a certain imagination to be able to think that a moon could be covered in mice. But, for that matter, it also takes imagination to recognize that it's covered in ice.

Br. Guy didn't come up with that idea himself. His master's thesis at MIT back in the 1970s was to explain *why* Europa was covered in ice. Other Jovian moons were known to be icy, too, but Europa was specifically "covered in ice"—that is, a body made primarily of rock and iron but with a relatively thin layer of ice on the surface.

The idea he was testing went like this: There would be plenty of the radioactive elements present in all that rocky moon material and those elements would decay, giving off heat, just as happens inside Earth. That's what gives us the heat that melts lavas and produces volcanoes. If there was also water ice mixed in with the rock inside that moon, the idea went, enough heat would be produced in the rocks to melt any interior ice. Once the ice melted, the rock would settle downward, and the water would flow upward to the surface of the moon—Aristotle would understand this—and cover it with whitish-colored, highly reflective ice, with maybe a liquid ocean beneath the ice. In any event, all the rock would be covered by the ice. That would make Europa, interestingly, the sort of water-covered world that medieval thinkers thought the Earth should be.

But did this idea really make sense, scientifically? Or did it just sound good, like other ideas we have encountered in previous chapters? The young Guy (a few decades before he became "Brother") was tasked by his academic advisor, Prof. John Lewis, with trying to understand this better. Guy used a room-sized computer called an IBM 360 to calculate the heat produced inside the moon against the heat flowing out of the moon's surface, to see if the idea could really work. He had to write a program (an *app* would be the word used today) for the IBM 360 to model the heat flow and keep track of how much heat was available to melt the ice. He wrote his moon heat model using a programming language called FORTRAN IV and stored it not on a hard disk or a USB drive or "in the cloud," but on a large stack of sturdy paper cards with holes punched in them. (The holes in the cards were the information read by the computer; this was a long time ago!)

But notice something here. To create this model, he already had to know that Europa and the other moons of Jupiter that he was studying were made of a mixture of rock and ice. Indeed, one of the major variables from moon to moon was how much rock it contained, and thus, how much heat it generated; the more rock, the more radioactive elements inside the rock, and the more heat there would be from the decay of those elements to melt the ice.

Wait a minute! How could anyone know what was inside a moon orbiting Jupiter, especially in a case like Europa, where somehow it was already known that most of the supposed rock was hidden, covered up beneath an ice crust? How did they know that—especially since this was before any spacecraft had ever visited that Jupiter satellite? (A long time ago, as we said.)

Guy didn't know for himself. He was just an undergraduate when he started this project, and so he relied on what his advisor, Prof. Lewis, had apprised him of—the then-current state of knowledge. How did Prof. Lewis know? Not only was this a few years before any spacecraft had visited those moons, but when Guy was starting this work, no one had even been able to use Earth-based telescopes to detect the spectrum, the luminous signature, of ice from the Jovian moons. (The first such detections of water ice on those moons happened while he was in the middle of his project.)

Why did anyone back then think that Jupiter's moons were made of rock and ice?

It never occurred to Guy to even ask. Perhaps too often, scientists do not think to ask such questions. As Fr. George V. Coyne, SJ, once said (the long-time director of the Vatican Observatory whom we met in the last chapter, and a later mentor to Br. Guy), if you question everything in science, you'll never *do* anything.

And yet, if you do ask those questions, you sometimes uncover some remarkable stories of scientists thinking up ideas that make Harry Potter's idea of a moon covered with *mice* look a little less bizarre.

WHEN SCIENCE GOES WRONG

It turns out that you can use three bits of knowledge to recognize that the moons of Jupiter should be icy. One is knowledge of their *brightnesses*. Ice is very bright—that is, it reflects much light. Think of a blanket of snow on a sunny day, especially compared to something like a layer of fresh asphalt. An object with high reflectivity (the term astronomers use is *albedo*) might suggest ice to an astronomer. Finding a moon's albedo should be simple. You look at the moon through the telescope. You measure how big it is. You see how bright it looks. If it reflects a lot of light for its size, then it has a high albedo...making you think "ice."

Another clue was knowledge of the moons' *densities*. Ice is much less dense than rock, so a lower-than-expected density might suggest ice. Finding a moon's density should not be too tough. Density is mass divided by volume; a cubic centimeter of rock weighs roughly three grams, while a cubic centimeter of ice weighs less than one. (A cubic centimeter of iron weighs about eight.) The moon's volume will be easy once you measure the size—the same measurement used for its brightness, but now that diameter is used to calculate the volume of the moon as a sphere (remembering the formula from high school geometry). Then, if you can measure the mass of the moon, you can calculate its density. If the density is ice-like, you think "ice." If it is rock-like, you think "rock." If it is between ice and rock, you can think a "mixture of ice and rock."

But wait—these are moons orbiting Jupiter, which is an entirely different world from Earth. Why think "ice," and not "strange Jupiter material"? Couldn't the moons be made from some exotic space material that could also be low in density but high in albedo? Isn't this extrapolating (as we have discussed) a little too far? That's the third bit of information you need.

In the nineteenth century, pioneers in astrophysics like Fr. Angelo Secchi, SJ, figured out how to insert a glass prism into their telescopes to split the light from stars into a rainbow of colors. Secchi located his telescope in the observatory that he built atop the Church of St. Ignatius of Loyola in Rome—an observatory that was a predecessor of the Vatican Observatory. Secchi used that rainbow spectrum to determine what elements are present in stars—different atoms and molecules produce subtly different patterns within the rainbow; each has its own luminous signature. He identified the spectral signature of hydrogen gas in the light of many different stars. By the early twentieth century, astronomers understood that all stars are made of mostly hydrogen, with helium coming in a distant second. The most common elements after hydrogen and helium are oxygen, carbon, and nitrogen.

Assuming that the planets are made from the same pot of ingredients as the stars, one can then further assume—extrapolate—that the most common compounds in planets and their moons should turn out to be water, methane, and ammonia, since these are the chemicals made when hydrogen reacts with oxygen, with carbon, and with nitrogen, respectively. And, in fact, that's what you find in the gas giant planets of our solar system—Jupiter through Neptune. So, the extrapolation seems to work there. Of course, the inner planets like Earth and Mars are just made of rocks, so presumably that's what's left over if all the gas goes away. And after all, those rocky planets are indeed much smaller than the gas giants, consistent with this idea.

(If you are feeling leery about all this extrapolation, good for you! This line of thought also led to the idea that there would be no planets—recall from chapter 1—of size between Venus–Earth and Uranus–Neptune. That did not work out.)

In the outer solar system, compounds like water, methane, and ammonia will all be cold enough that they should all freeze into ices. The easiest to freeze is water—we have snow and ice even on Earth, at temperatures where methane and ammonia are still gases. It's also likely to be the most abundant since there's more oxygen found in stars' spectra than carbon or nitrogen. Therefore, it's reasonable to identify the low-density, high-brightness material in the moons of Jupiter as water ice.

SEZIONE PROSPETTICA INTERNA DEL CIELO MOBILE E DELL' EQUATORIALE DI MERZ

Fig. 4A. At top is Fr. Secchi's telescope, housed in the observatory he built atop the church of St. Ignatius in Rome. A large dome intended for St. Ignatius had never been built, so Secchi put the church's strong structure to the purpose of supporting an observatory instead of that dome. At bottom is a sketch of Saturn that Secchi produced.

Images from the library of the Vatican Observatory.

In fact, by the latter half of the nineteenth century, astronomers mostly had the knowledge needed to recognize that the moons of Jupiter should be icy: they knew that hydrogen and oxygen were common in stars; they could measure the sizes of the moons; they could even estimate how much mass each moon had. Together, all of that should have pointed to the moons orbiting Jupiter being balls of ice, or ice and rock. But it turns out that a lot of science would go wrong before astronomers actually put these ideas together and figured out that the moons should be icy.

One place to see the state of knowledge among astronomers is in the books they write for popular audiences. Consider the 1873 edition of Rev. Thomas W. Webb's *Celestial Objects for Common Telescopes*, and Simon Newcomb's widely read 1877 book, *Popular Astronomy*. What they say about Jupiter's moons, and about astronomy in the nineteenth century, is surprising.

Take, for instance, what they say about the brightnesses of Jupiter's moons. You might think astronomers could just look at a moon through the telescope and measure how big it is and see how bright it looks. According to Newcomb, however, "the light of these satellites varies to an extent which it is difficult to account for, except by supposing very violent changes constantly going on on their surfaces." Now that is an interesting science-gone-wrong twist! Nobody talks about such brightness fluctuations today. Nobody sees any such thing. Where did Newcomb get this idea? He was an accomplished astronomer. He was at the U.S. Naval Observatory, among other things. He should have been a reputable source.

But Webb also goes on at length citing different people who all saw radical changes in the brightness of these moons. For example, about Jupiter's moon Callisto, Rev. Webb writes, "As far back as 1707 Maraldi noticed that, though usually faintest, it was sometimes brightest (a variation which he ascribes to all the satellites); in 1711 Bianchini and another once saw it for more than 1h so feeble that it could hardly be perceived; 1849, June 13 Lassell made a similar observation with far superior means." He also cites other notable astronomers, including the German astronomer Rudolf Engelmann; the Englishman John Herschel; and the famous lunar observers Beer and Mädler; and even Secchi in Rome—who also describe seeing the *shapes* of these moons being "irregular and elliptical; and according to the Roman observers, the ellipse does not always line the same way." Indeed, various observers of that era reported spots, bright equatorial regions, and other features on their surfaces.

What are the odds that these astronomers were actually seeing real features on those moons? Not good. Telescopes have an inherent limit in their ability to resolve detail, a sort of natural "pixel size" that depends on the width of the main lens and the wavelength of the light. (This is the same effect that makes pinpoint stars look like fuzzy disks, as we described in chapter 1.) The main lens of Secchi's telescope atop the Church of St. Ignatius measured just under ten inches wide, meaning its natural "pixel size" was about half of an arc second.

An "arc second" is a measure of size in the sky. There are 360 degrees in a circle; 60 arc minutes to a degree; and 60 arc seconds to an arc minute. For comparison, the apparent width of the full moon is half a degree, which is 30 arc minutes, or 1800 arc seconds.

Thus, Secchi's "pixel size" was about 1/3600 of the width of the full moon. Ganymede, Jupiter's largest moon, never appears larger than 1.8 arc seconds in diameter, or 1/1000 of the full moon. So, through Secchi's telescope, you would expect it to be only about four pixels wide, at best.

Four pixels cannot show much. However, planetary observers in that era always patiently awaited the rare moments when the atmosphere overhead was the most clear and still, and if the object was bright and the magnification very strong—certainly the case for these moons—at these times they could have recognized features that pushed the limits of what astronomers thought were possible for a telescope. After all, the diameters they reported for these moons were not all that bad, good to within 10 percent of the actual value—a precision of about a tenth of an arc second.

Secchi, however, reports the diameter of these moons to a precision of one-*thousandth* of an arc second, and one of his Jovian moon drawings features what appear to be polar caps like those seen on Mars! Such caps do not exist. Even Webb, who was admirably cautious about reporting what other people claimed to have seen, writes, "I have sometimes noticed differences in the sizes of the discs which I thought were not imaginary." This, using just a *six-inch aperture* telescope! People today have telescopes of that size that they received as gifts, gathering dust in their closets. Nice telescopes, but very limited. This is a case of imagination gone a little wild.

The favorite theory of those days for these strange fluctuations was that these moons were shaped like pancakes and tumbling: one moment astronomers might see the moons edge-on and dim, and then later, face-on and bright; and when in between edge-on and face-on, the moons would look like ellipses. Regardless of how strange this explanation might sound to us, astronomers did think they were seeing significant brightness changes. Those changes would make it hard to look at the sizes of Jupiter's moons, and their brightnesses, to notice that they had ice-like albedos.

Things were no better when it came to the densities of those moons. Finding the mass of a moon is very difficult. It is easy to use the orbital period of a moon to calculate the mass of the planet it is orbiting—if the *planet* is more massive, the moon orbits more quickly. But this tells you nothing about the mass of the moon itself, which is what we need. Recall what we saw Locher and Fr. Scheiner (and Newton) say about objects in orbit: an orbit is just the path of a moon as it falls around its planet. And as Galileo showed when he dropped the two differing weights from the tower of Pisa, all objects, heavy or light, fall at the same rate in the same gravity field (if they don't flutter in the air like a piece of paper). So that means that any moon, regardless of mass, in a given orbit will fall around the planet at the same rate.

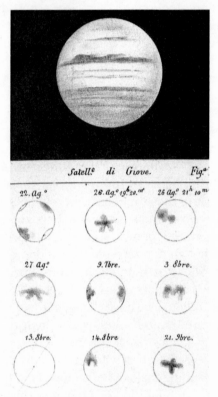

Fig. 4B. Secchi's sketches of Jupiter (top) and of features supposedly visible on its moons (bottom). The top-left moon sketch shows what appear to be polar caps, such as exist on Earth and are seen on Mars.

Images from the library of the Vatican Observatory.

However, if more than one moon is orbiting the planet, as is the case with Jupiter, then you can measure how each moon pulls on the other moons, subtly deflecting their orbits, and from that you can work out the mass of each from those pulls. That is a complicated mathematical problem, but Pierre Simon Laplace did it in 1805...probably with the help of some really good computers.

By "computers," we don't mean IBM 360s, or the latest elegant-looking desktop machines from Apple. We mean *human* computers; people who were truly talented, and very fast, at mathematics. Prior to the advent of electronic computers, it was just such people who did the sort of heavy calculation work involved in something like looking at many precision measurements of Jupiter's moons and determining from those measurements just how much those moons were pulling on each other. Thanks to the movie *Hidden Figures*, and the women who were human computers in the early days of NASA that the movie (and book) portrays, the idea of human computers is more familiar to people today. Many of those NASA human computers, such as Katherine Johnson, went on to become pioneers in the use of early electronic computers like the IBM 360 that Guy used, with the punch cards.

The Vatican Observatory has itself benefitted from the work of human computers. One of the observatory's first major undertakings was participation in the *Carte du Ciel* project, an international effort to photographically catalog and map the heavens. In 1906, Pope Pius X, seeing that the observatory's work on the project was stalling, called on Archbishop Pietro Maffi of Pisa to reorganize the observatory. Maffi found Fr. John Hagen, whom we met in the last chapter. Hagen had never been involved in a project that required so much measurement and calculations, so he consulted with other observatories and quickly figured out that he needed some good computers, and that many observatories were hiring women for the job ("lady computers" they were called at the Royal Observatory in Greenwich, England). Maffi helped Hagen find computers from among the ranks of the Sisters of the Holy Child Mary, who were located near the Vatican. Sisters Emilia Ponzoni, Regina Colombo, Concetta Finardi, and Luigia Panceri would all work as computers for the Vatican Observatory. From 1910 to 1921, they measured and cataloged 481,215 stars from hundreds of glass photographic plates.

Fig. 4C. Sisters of the Holy Child Mary, working to measure and catalog stars from glass photographic plates from the *Carte du Ciel* project.

Image from the collections of the Vatican Observatory.

At the time, the sisters were recognized for their work. The Vatican's ten-volume contribution to the catalog cited them and complimented their "alacrity," "diligence," and "zeal." In the 1920s, Popes Benedict XV and Pius XI each met with them and gave them gifts in recognition of their work.

But then the "sister computers," much like the women of *Hidden Figures*, were largely forgotten, only to be "rediscovered" in the twenty-first century.

Perhaps human computers were forgotten in part because of the march of technological progress. Perhaps once their work was automated and the job of "computer" eliminated, it was hard to see them as important. Be that as it may, one way in which science has consistently gone wrong over time, and suffered from a failure of imagination, is in how it has tended to focus on its "big names" like Laplace, and to overlook the many, many others whose contributions to the scientific endeavor have also been crucial. If no one does the tedious calculations, we don't find the masses of the moons.

Laplace had found the mass of each moon by 1805. He was able to determine those masses to within 10 to 25 percent of the currently accepted values. That was not bad, for an age of no electronic computers!

With Laplace's moon masses, and with moon sizes measured by Fr. Secchi and others, astronomers could calculate moon densities. But they didn't. The popular astronomy books mentioned earlier would happily list the size and the mass of each moon. But none of them would bother to divide the mass by the volume to calculate a density!

Why didn't astronomers find that answer? Because they never asked that question. Prior to Secchi, astronomers were just not interested in knowing what stars and planets were made from. Friedrich Wilhelm Bessel, for example, said that astronomy "must lay down the rules for determining the *motions* of the heavenly bodies as they appear to us from the Earth" but other information about heavenly bodies—like density—was, he said, "not properly of astronomical interest." That meant that even with the data right in front of them, people like him might not even have thought to ask about the compositions of these moons. Even Secchi, in his pioneering

1852 book on planetary physics, *The Physical Framework of the Solar System*, only lists the moons' sizes and masses without calculating their densities.

Astronomers just didn't ask that question, except for George Chambers, a science popularizer in London. His 1861 *A Handbook of Descriptive and Practical Astronomy* contains a wonderful table of sizes, masses...and *densities* of the Jupiter moons. Hurrah for Chambers!

However, his densities look very odd; they are all only about *a tenth* the density of water. What in nature has such a density? Stuff that floats in water, like most types of wood, different kinds of oil, or even water ice, typically have densities that are not much less than water. Rock, of course, is denser than ice. However, gases have densities a thousandth that of water. There is hardly anything in nature with a density between ice and air—of one-tenth that of water. Maybe balsa wood? Yet Chambers doesn't notice this. He just lists the numbers, without comment.

And what's weird is that the numbers he uses in his table for the sizes and masses of the moons are reasonably good. He should have computed densities that were not too far from the numbers we use today, suggesting icy moons. But somehow, he just didn't get the arithmetic right. Maybe he didn't employ good "computers."

In thinking to calculate the densities for Jupiter's moons, Chambers alone of his peers was on the right path. He was *almost* there. But then, with his bad math, published with no concern for whether his densities made any sense, he went astray. And, like the other astronomers of his epoch, he never used any of these data to speculate about the composition of those moons. "Not properly of astronomical interest," perhaps.

Chambers, like Secchi and others of this time, seems to have suffered from a failure of imagination that held back the progress of science. They had information needed to at least make good guesses about what Jupiter's moons were made of. They just did not think to take that next step that seems so logical to us today.

The first person we can find who made careful (and correct) measurements of both the brightnesses and densities of Jupiter's moons and took the next step to consider what they meant, was Edward Pickering, the director of the Harvard College Observatory. In a paper published in 1907, Pickering gives tables of diameters, densities, and albedos for each of the moons; and (finally!) his values aren't all that far from what we know today from spacecraft measurements.

First, Pickering reports the intrinsic brightness of each of the moons. In the 1870s, he had developed a technique that measured how much he needed to dim the light of Jupiter with filters to match the moons' observed brightnesses. Using diameters from an 1871 book by Rudolf Engelmann (which, amusingly enough, reports the moons' diameters to ridiculous degrees of precision, much like Secchi), Pickering came up with albedos for the moons. His albedos were only about half the modern accepted values; but still, he calculated that Europa is about twice as reflective as Earth's moon.

And what is more exciting is what Pickering did *not* see. In the 1879 *Annals of the Harvard College Observatory*, he wrote, "It has been thought by many astronomers that the light of the satellites of Jupiter was variable. This view is not sustained by the present measurements....During the past two or three years, I have frequently had occasion to compare the satellites, and in no case have I been able to perceive any marked change in their relative brightness beyond that due to the proximity of Jupiter."

"The proximity of Jupiter!" That's what had led the other astronomers astray. When you look at Europa through the eyepiece of your telescope, you are likely to have a certain bright object right next to it in the eyepiece: Jupiter. If you don't have

Pickering's technique of filtering Jupiter's light, but not Europa's, then your eye will adjust to the brightness of Jupiter, and Europa will seem dimmer as a result! But when Europa is farther away from Jupiter, it will seem brighter.

Pickering's explanation for the variable light of the moons had, in fact, been proposed 250 years earlier, shortly after they were first discovered, by Scheiner and Locher (yes, them again). They wrote about the effect of Jupiter's brilliance on the eye and on the perceived brightnesses of its moons in their 1614 book, *Mathematical Disquisitions*—they seem to have had something to say about everything astronomical in that book. "Anyone who can see, has seen a lesser light obscured by a greater; a weaker, by a stronger," Locher and Scheiner wrote. Or rather: *Obfuscari autem lucidum minus a maiore, debilius a fortiore, qui non vidit, nihil vidit*, since Latin was the language of science in 1614. Perhaps this is the reason that the nineteenth-century astronomers seem not to have known about their analysis—when we lose contact with past scientists, we lose knowledge.

Pickering even interpreted the data he saw in his table. "It will be noted that the densities...are extremely small for solid bodies," he wrote. "The density of our moon, which is of about their size is 3.44 [times the density of water], and that of the Earth much larger." And then, with density and albedo measurements in hand, he proceeded to suggest what the moons might be made of: "Their density and brightness are what we should expect if they were composed of"—*Wait for it!*—"loose heaps of white sand."

(Surely, you were not expecting the right answer here. This is, after all, a book about science gone wrong!)

But why sand? Why didn't Pickering even think of ice?

For one thing, though Secchi had found hydrogen in stars, the idea that the universe was *mostly* hydrogen had not yet been generally accepted. Pickering wouldn't necessarily have expected ice to be a common substance in space.

Additionally, he was convinced that the moons actually could not be solid because, as he explains, unless the moons are made of something that can change shape like sand, "it is impossible to understand how rigid bodies could assume the varying ellipticities exhibited by these bodies...the variations of whose shape follow no obvious law."

Remember those earlier astronomers who talked about the moons being "irregular and elliptical"? Sand spinning very fast would flatten itself into a pancake shape—that strange shape that the earlier astronomers had required to explain the rapid changes in the moons' brightnesses—*the very changes that Pickering's own work had told him did not actually happen!*

Pickering's conclusion may be a great example of science gone wrong, in ironic fashion, but you can't say that he suffered from failure of imagination. A moon that is a spinning loose heap of white sand is almost as imaginative as Harry Potter's moon covered in mice.

It wasn't until about 1923 that the actual natures of the Jovian moons were finally worked out by the great geophysicist Harold Jeffreys. "The densities are comparable with the density of ice," he wrote in a paper that was published in the *Astrophysical Journal*. That was about fifty years after astronomers could have, and arguably should have, gotten the correct answer, given the data they already had, and only fifty years before the spectral signature of ice on the Jovian moons' surfaces was finally confirmed, as the young Guy Consolmagno was studying those moons.

Of course, Jeffreys was calculating the composition of the moons of Jupiter to support his idea that Jupiter itself was mostly made of ice. He didn't consider how the enormous internal pressure of a body as big as Jupiter would compress ice—or the gaseous hydrogen that we now recognize makes up the bulk of Jupiter.

Still, that is how, when Br. Guy was doing his master's thesis, astronomers knew that Jupiter's moons were made of rock and ice. With his thesis, Guy would make his own contribution to our understanding of Jupiter's moons. He would also contribute his own failure of imagination.

At the end of his thesis about heat generated from radioactivity in the moons melting ices inside them, Guy wrote,

> Given the temperatures of the interiors, and especially of the silicate layers through which liquid will be percolating, the possibility exists of simple organic chemistry taking place, involving either methane from the ice or carbon in the silicate phase. However, we stop short of postulating life forms in these mantles; we leave such to others more experienced than ourselves in such speculations.

Note the royal "we." What you are reading is actually a rather snide comment from a twenty-two-year-old kid! Who was Guy thinking would be "more experienced" in such speculations? Carl Sagan. Sagan was the only scientist seriously searching for life on other planets, and his work was subject to significant skepticism (and scorn) from the scientific community. *Not properly of interest.* Sagan was also famous—some would say notorious—for postulating various unlikely places in the solar system where life might exist.

Guy's very first scientific presentation was a week after he turned in that thesis. It was at a meeting about Jupiter hosted at the University of Arizona, where he had just arrived to begin his doctoral work. He presented the last paper of the opening session. The chair of the session was...Carl Sagan.

Before Guy spoke, he mentioned to Sagan this idea of life in the oceans. He figured Sagan might be intrigued about yet another place to look for life. But Sagan looked skeptical. "Life needs sunlight for energy," he said, "and those oceans would be under a thick ice layer; it will be pitch dark in them. No sunlight will reach there. No chance for life."

Guy felt chagrined and foolish. This was so obvious, and he had missed it. And so, during his talk, he did not mention life in those oceans at all. Nor did he bring up the subject again in any of the papers he wrote on his models of those moons.

Some years later, though, life forms were found in the deepest, darkest parts of Earth's oceans. Creatures like tube worms can live off the energy not of sunlight, but of volcanic plumes on the ocean floors. And soon thereafter, a group of scientists put that discovery together with the thought of oceans in Europa to talk about life there. Today, it's a hot topic to search for possible life under the ice of Europa, or Saturn's icy moon, Enceladus, or other icy moons. Ideas for probes to explore for life on Europa are on the drawing board at NASA. Like George Chambers in the nineteenth century, Guy had been *almost* there—*almost* correct—about Jupiter's moons.

The story of ice on Jupiter's moons, or of water under the ice, illustrates how science can go wrong through failure of imagination. Astronomers faced great difficulties in determining the masses and sizes of the Jovian moons. Yet what held them back from understanding what those moons were made of was not those difficulties. Their failure came in not looking for things that were "not of proper interest," so that, even when astronomers had the masses and sizes of the moons in hand, they did not think to determine their densities—or if they did think to determine their densities, they did not care to check their math, or think about whether their answers made any sense at all. Science benefits from scientists having the imagination to, as the cliché goes, "think outside the box." But, as we have described, science is also a social activity and asking the questions that the other astronomers weren't asking comes with a social cost.

It takes not only imagination but courage to consider what things that we usually do not take interest in might be within the grasp of our knowledge. That's the kind of imagination that lets us envision whirling moons made of sand, or maybe even tube worms (if not mice) on Europa.

Chapter 5

The Cult of "Intelligence"

There are, of course, the times in our history when science has gone wrong in horrifying ways. The science-gone-wrong stories of the first four chapters of this book are all from astronomy. That is because the authors of this book are astronomers. Those stories—of weird ideas about our place in the universe, or the nature of our world, or of Jupiter's moons—are amusing, not horrifying. They are also stories that we authors know much about; they all pertain to the research of one or both of us.

But a book about science gone wrong should discuss how it has gone wrong in ways that are not amusing—that are far more consequential and disturbing than Jupiter's moons being made of white sand. That means we authors of this book have had to get outside of our area of expertise, to consider not the scientific measurement and study of the heavens (astronomy), but the scientific (supposedly) measurement and study of... human beings.

Before you picked up this book, you perhaps had never heard of Ptolemy, Genesis, and the sizes of the moon and stars.

WHEN SCIENCE GOES WRONG

You maybe had never heard of the Two Spheres Theory. But you probably had heard about the Scopes "Monkey Trial," the public fight over the teaching of evolution in public schools in Dayton, Tennessee.

There, in 1925, lawyers Clarence Darrow and William Jennings Bryan duked it out in front of a packed courthouse, in what became a 1920s media circus. Heather Gilligan, a journalist and editor at timeline.com, has described how the Scopes trial has been portrayed as "the ultimate fight between science and religion," in which "science won"...except that, as she points out, it wasn't, and it didn't.

Gilligan writes, "The real Scopes story...isn't quite as simple as a parable about enlightened science versus close-minded religion."[1] Science-versus-religion stories never are so simple, even though there is a small industry busy saying otherwise. Getting history right is always a challenge. What *Inherit the Wind* and all the other dramatizations about the Scopes trial leave out is that the evolution textbook used by Scopes also claimed that evolution "explained" the so-called natural superiority of certain races and nationalities. Worse, it promoted eugenics—creating better human beings through "good breeding."

You can read *Civic Biology* for yourself; it is available on Google Books. There you can see, if you have the stomach for it, a book that is very explicit about eugenics. It uses the word *eugenics*; it openly cheerleads for it. It describes the poor, the handicapped, and the insane as "true parasites," and it adds, regarding a "remedy" for these parasites:

> If such people were lower animals, we would prob-
> ably kill them off to prevent them from spreading.

---

1. Heather Gilligan, "The Most Famous Textbook in American History Is Full of Garbage Science," timeline.org, January 30, 2017, https://timeline.com/evolution -scopes-trial-eugenics-6bbdb9f7515a.

Humanity will not allow this, but we do have the remedy of separating the sexes in asylums and in various ways preventing intermarriage and the possibilities of perpetuating such a low and degenerate race.

The supporters of eugenics used Darwin's new theory of evolution as an excuse to support and justify their beliefs. And while there is nothing in the biological theory itself that demands such an interpretation, it could be easily read into how Darwin himself presented it. Gilligan writes,

[William Jennings Bryan] was aghast at the eugenics baked into Darwin's theory of evolution, which had already resulted in policies like state-sponsored forced sterilizations of people of color and others considered undesirable in the decades before the trial.

Bryan planned to cover his objections to eugenics in his closing statement, but he never got to deliver one. The defense, in a surprise move, declined their right to a closing statement, which meant Bryan also had to forego his. He'd planned to read from parts of Darwin's work to make his point, including this sentence from *The Descent of Man*: "It is surprising how soon a want of care, or care wrongly directed, leads to the degeneration of a domestic race; but, excepting in the case of man himself, hardly anyone is so ignorant as to allow his worst animals to breed." Darwin, he'd intended to say, "reveals the barbarous sentiment that runs through evolution and dwarfs the moral nature of those who become obsessed with it."

Eugenics was not the only kind of barbarous sentiment that science had produced regarding human beings by the time of the Scopes trial. Even before Darwin, various scientists had argued for "polygenism" against "monogenism" or the "unity of man." Monogenism held that all people had a common origin—all were of one family, all "sons of Adam and daughters of Eve," to borrow a phrase from C. S. Lewis. People from central Africa differed from those from northern Europe who differed from those from Mexico for reasons of environment and long-term geographic separation, and nothing more.

But polygenists couldn't believe that environment and separation could explain the differences between human "races" and insisted instead that these different groups had separate origins and distinct characteristics. They were different "species." These species could not beget viable offspring, polygenists claimed, at least not over the long term. The hybrid, infertile offspring of a horse and a donkey was termed a "mule"; regarding people, their term was *mulatto*. According to Josiah C. Nott and George Glidden in their mid-nineteenth-century book *Types of Mankind* (of which numerous editions were published), these suffered from infertility over the long term, and would die off over a short span of generations. Therefore, they concluded, the world is peopled by fixed types of mankind.

Today ideas like these are often labeled as "pseudoscience." They were not "pseudo" at the time, however. They were science gone very wrong.

The American Association for the Advancement of Science (AAAS) is one of the premier scientific societies in the world, and its journal, *Science*, is considered one of the most prestigious. Josiah C. Nott was an early member of the AAAS. In 1850, at the AAAS meeting in Charleston, South Carolina, he gave a paper citing the Jewish "race" as evidence for long-term fixity of type and against the unity of mankind. His talk included mention of the varying degrees of intelligence in the various types of man.

Another AAAS member, Louis Agassiz, who three years earlier had arrived with acclaim from Switzerland to take up a professorship at Harvard, then offered some remarks on Nott's paper. Agassiz noted, "Viewed zoologically, the several races of men were well marked and distinct"; and it was clear that "the differences we notice at present between the races" were very old.[2] Furthermore, at the same AAAS meeting, this prominent scientist claimed that it was clear that "these races did not originate from a common centre, nor from a single pair"—they were *not* all of one family; *not* all sons of Adam and daughters of Eve. And with an interesting blast of concordism that was common with polygenists, Agassiz noted that this "did not militate against the teachings of Scripture History," since the Bible states that "as early as the days of Cain, there were other lands already peopled, in which the wanderer took refuge" (see Genesis 4:14–17, in which Cain goes off the to the land of Nod, and takes a wife).

These kinds of ideas about human beings were part and parcel of the public face of science in the late nineteenth and early twentieth centuries. Consider actual scientists like Alexander Graham Bell; popularizers like H. G. Wells; and legal experts such as the U.S. Supreme Court Chief Justice Oliver Wendell Holmes. They all weighed in on what they believed was the best science of the day and what it was describing. And they all promoted the idea of eugenics. They insisted that we could perfect the human race, or the individual "races," by encouraging good breeding of people. It was an idea so self-evident to them that anyone (like the Church) who opposed it on moral grounds was seen as dangerously backward.

Alexander Graham Bell was one of the leading scientists

---

2. What both men said was recorded in the published *Proceedings* of the 1850 meeting.

of his day, not just the inventor of the telephone. He was key to establishing the journal *Science*. His opinions reflected those of scientists across disciplines. In a 1908 article in *National Geographic*, he asked whether "we can formulate practical plans that might lead to the breeding of better men and better women." Noting that "superior individuals on the whole have a larger proportion of superior offspring than the average of the race," Bell suggested that, for the "improvement of the species," a "simple process of promoting the marriage of the superior with the superior" would be wise. He also suggested immigration restrictions, for eugenics purposes:

> A new people [is] being gradually evolved in the United States by the mingling together of the different races of the world in varying proportions. It is of the greatest consequence to us that the final result should be the evolution of a higher and nobler type of man in America, and not deterioration of the nation. To this end the process of evolution should be carefully studied, and then controlled by suitable immigration laws tending to eliminate undesirable ethnical elements, and to stimulate the admission of elements assimilated readily by our population and that tend to raise the standard of manhood here.

In 1924, the U.S. Congress did pass such a law. It put a strict quota on immigration from southern and eastern Europe: Poles and Italians were considered "undesirable," and after 1924, immigration from Italy to the United States fell by 90 percent. Worse, the act banned *all* immigration from Asia.

We remember H. G. Wells as a prolific science fiction writer, but in fact, he was even more influential as a science popularizer. He was a socialist and pacifist, whom standard internet biographies repeatedly describe as "a forward-looking, even prophetic social critic who devoted his literary talents to the development of a progressive vision on a global scale." He was famous in his time for his utopian works and his popularization of history, notably his two-volume *Outline of History* published in the 1920s.

He claimed to be antiracist and opposed to the idea of "positive eugenics" (breeding superior people); but he did support the idea that certain classes of people should be prevented from having children. In his 1906 *Socialism and the Family*, he wrote, "The children people bring into the world can be no more their private concern entirely, than the disease germs they disseminate or the noises a man makes in a thin-floored flat," and so the socialist state should be concerned about "disease and evil births alike." In his view, it was "sterilization of failures" that would improve the "human stock." His ideas became more nuanced with time; but his early books, with their more naïve vision of social engineering, continued to be popular well after his death.

Supreme Court Chief Justice Holmes is honored as a "progressive" voice on many topics such as the freedom of speech, and so his support of eugenics gave support to that idea among intellectuals (who naturally saw themselves as being "superior"). More specifically, his support for eugenics affected the rise of eugenic principles in the law itself. Under his direction, the U.S. Supreme Court in 1927 ruled 8-1 in *Buck vs. Bell* that forced sterilization on eugenic principles did not violate the Equal Protection Clause of the fourteenth amendment. He wrote, "It is better for all the world, if instead of waiting to execute degenerate offspring for crime, or to let them starve for their imbecility, society can prevent those who are manifestly unfit from continuing their kind." This decision is sometimes cited as one of the worst in U.S. Supreme Court history, but it has never been specifically reversed. Following the *Buck vs. Bell* decision, tens of thousands of women (mostly minorities) were forcibly sterilized in the United States in the name of eugenics. Such sterilization programs continued well into the 1970s.

Wells may have advocated for the sterilization of certain kinds of people—of "failures," he said—but today the combination of abortion and prenatal testing can work to make such ideas moot, by preventing certain kinds of people from ever being born in the first place. People with Down Syndrome are now regularly aborted; in some countries, they are all aborted. Abortion and prenatal testing threaten others who might not measure up, too. What would Wells and the other advocates for eugenics have thought of this ability to measure and assess people in the womb? Scopes's textbook stated that "humanity" would not allow for killing off those who failed to measure up, but it is clear that when science goes wrong, "humanity" can be a flexible concept. When we do not remember that people are beings of immeasurable worth, children of God, created in God's own image, and thus (to repurpose the sneering words of a certain nineteenth-century scientist whom we shall meet in a moment) "an exceptional instance in the grand scheme of creation," our science can go wrong in horrible ways.

And let's re-emphasize how *scientifically* wrong—not just repugnant—it all was. Promoters of eugenics developed tools to statistically analyze masses of data about people and demonstrate conclusively that their ideas worked, only to find those tools showed that their ideas about human beings were wrong. The complexity of the human genetic code makes any attempt to achieve an "improvement of the species" through "promoting the marriage of the superior with the superior" hopelessly naïve. All those ideas about polygenism and races and types of human beings have also turned out to be as wrong as the Two Spheres Theory. Today the science of genetics tells us that human beings are a single, and rather homogeneous, species. Different groups did not spring out of the ground or evolve separately; we are all, says science today, of one family, all descended from the same parents.

It's worth reflecting on how those who promoted the science of measuring people also promoted the idea of a warfare between science, on the march and working to show the world the truth, and religion, in retreat and bent on covering it all up. In their above-mentioned book, *Types of Mankind*, Nott and Glidden wrote,

> Scientific truth, exemplified in the annals of Astronomy, Geology, Chronology, Geographical distribution of animals, &c., has literally fought its way inch by inch through false theology. The last grand battle between science and dogmatism, on the primitive origin of races, has now commenced. It requires no prophetic eye to foresee that science must again, and finally, triumph.

And of course, *Types of Mankind* also references Galileo and the opposition he received from the theologians.

Likewise, in an article in the 1865 *Anthropological Review*, published by the Royal Anthropological Institute of Great Britain and Ireland, Georges Pouchet of the *Muséum national d'Histoire naturelle* in Paris wrote that "the battle fought and won by astronomy in the days of Galileo, was in truth but the beginning of the war, and alone would have proved utterly inadequate to teach men of science their strength, or theologians their weakness."

Pouchet (who is that certain nineteenth-century scientist mentioned a moment ago) proceeded to discuss why the meddling of theologians, with their notions that human beings were "an exceptional instance in the grand scheme of creation, an isolated phenomenon in the great plan of nature" (and thus of exceptional value), was "an impertinence that the dignity of science can afford to treat with the silent contempt it so richly deserves." Pouchet also went on to discuss whom science showed to be superior and inferior among human beings.

As it happens, the eugenicists lost their war. Science today fully supports traditional ideas about human beings being of one family. And for that matter, while traditional ideas about the immobility of the Earth that motivated opposition to Galileo may have been overthrown, they are still reflected in how even modern astronomers casually speak of the sun rising and setting. By contrast, no modern scientists speak casually of different species of human beings, or of the "breeding of better men and better women." Any who did would quickly be numbered among the ranks of the more unpleasant crackpots. People like Nott and Pouchet lost that war so badly that today their work is called "pseudo" science, separating by words modern science from the science that, not so long ago, went so horribly wrong.

They should have known they were going wrong. Shakespeare told us long ago that those "on top" are not inherently superior to their fellow human beings:

> I think the king is but a man, as I am: the violet smells to him as it doth to me: the element shows to him as it doth to me; all his senses have but human conditions: his ceremonies laid by, in his nakedness he appears but a man; and though his affections are higher mounted than ours, yet, when they stoop, they stoop with the like wing. Therefore when he sees reason of fears, as we do, his fears, out of doubt, be of the same relish as ours are. (*Henry V*, Act 4, Scene 1)

St. Augustine tells us,

> Whoever is anywhere born a man, that is, a rational, mortal animal, no matter what unusual appearance

he presents in color, movement, sound, nor how peculiar he is in some power, part, or quality of his nature, no Christian can doubt that he springs from that one protoplast. (*City of God*, Book XVI)

And then, of course, there is this:

There is no longer Jew or Greek, there is no longer slave or free, there is no longer male and female; for all of you are one in Christ Jesus. (Galatians 3:28)

And this:

After this I looked, and there was a great multitude that no one could count, from every nation, from all tribes and peoples and languages, standing before the throne and before the Lamb, robed in white, with palm branches in their hands....Then one of the elders addressed me, saying....

"They will hunger no more, and thirst no more;
   the sun will not strike them,
   nor any scorching heat;
for the Lamb at the center of the throne will be
      their shepherd,
   and he will guide them to springs of the water of
      life,
and God will wipe away every tear from their eyes."
   (Revelation 7:9–17)

And if Shakespeare, Augustine, and the Bible were not sufficient to tell the Notts, Pouchets, and Bells of the world that they were going wrong, then arguably, common sense and experience should have sufficed. Any efforts to study and evaluate "superior" human beings would have to be flawed, since even the criteria that we would choose to measure any improvement would have to be flawed.

We cannot measure some form of "superiority" that would let us join "the superior with the superior" to breed people toward some imagined pinnacle of humanity in the way that we can measure human height and weight. Indeed, while the "eu" in "eugenics" is from the Greek for "good," what exactly would be the "good" that it's supposed to be looking for? The arguments about the abilities of different races, and about "improving" the human race as a whole, had implicit in them the unsurprising assumption that the best of humanity looked an awful lot like those who wanted to be directing the improving. This would seem to be confirmation bias at work; if you think that you yourself are the pinnacle of humanity, then *eu*-genics just becomes *you*-genics.

The fact is that we can't even measure people regarding more definable concepts, like athletic prowess. It would seem easy to determine who can run or bicycle or swim a certain distance in the least time, or jump the farthest or the highest, or score the most points in a tennis match. But it is not.

The simple measurement of who has the best times can become very controversial when someone tests positive for a banned substance, and who has the best times can be heavily influenced by who has the best gear. There is a constant struggle to ensure that sporting events are about the human spirit and not merely an arms race of technology. Most sporting authorities ban various clever advantages such as particular kinds of running shoes or swimsuits. Steroids and other performance enhancing drugs are also widely banned.

But what about the best practice facilities? Or the best coaching? Or the best support from an early age?

There are more than a billion people in India, and plenty of mountains with snow, but India has never won a medal in the winter Olympics. India doesn't have a culture that values those sports, or legions of moms and dads who encourage their kids to ski or skate, much less leagues with coaches where the kids could learn to compete or find jobs when their competitive days are over.

In tennis, "footwork"—knowing how to move about the court well—is very important; it is also easiest to learn when young. A person who is not introduced to a tennis racket until high school may never master those skills. Any individual player can do a lot through personal determination and talent, but overall, good tennis players are likely to come from places where there is a strong "culture of tennis" that provides all those things that help players be the best they can possibly be and does so at the best possible times in the players' developments.

Imagine that you are a eugenicist around the time of the Scopes trial, with an eye to produce better tennis through selective "breeding" of tennis-talented men and women. You have no moral qualms about this. You set to work like a livestock breeder, rationally measuring and observing the best tennis players of your time, hoping to promote the marriage of "the superior with the superior." What are the odds, do you think, that, out of your 1920s tennis playing "breed stock," you would ever produce a player who could play like Serena Williams? And of course, what made Serena Williams great was more than just physical attributes; her *style* of play was revolutionary for women's tennis. Indeed, what is missing from all this discussion is that the best athletes are distinguished beyond their physical skills by intangibles such as desire, leadership, emotional resilience, and their creative approaches to solve old problems in new ways.

Considering the difficulties involved in athletics, where times and scores are supposedly simple measurements, what of intelligence, something Josiah Nott was so interested in?

How do you measure it? There exist tests, with the average centered at 100, to try to put some sort of scale on measuring an "Intelligence Quotient," but they assume that "intelligence" is a single one-dimensional concept that can be measured objectively, with a single "IQ" number. A cynic might say that the only thing an IQ test can measure is how well a person can do on an IQ test.

Indeed, it is easy to demonstrate that the people who do well on IQ tests are those of a culture and background most like the people who develop those tests. Test designers are not going to create tests that they, and their "smart" friends, colleagues, and family members, are going to fail. And this isn't necessarily because of some conscious bias to rig the tests; it can result simply from an ignorance of how certain questions and concepts are understood across different cultures. The people who try to measure "smartness" aren't always very smart about it.

And the idea that intelligence can be measured by a single number is contrary to common sense when you have been around a variety of people. The authors of this book have taught at Harvard and MIT, and at community colleges. We don't deny that the students who are found in one sort of institution may have different skills, different abilities, different cultural assumptions, and different problems to be overcome than those at another. (That's as true about the difference separating MIT and Harvard students as it is about the difference separating either of these groups of students and community college students. That's why different colleges have different admission policies.) But we know firsthand that these differences cannot be ranked as "superior" or "inferior."

Br. Guy once got a lesson on this when he spent a semester teaching at Le Moyne College, a small Jesuit school in Syracuse, New York. It attracts many students who are older than traditional students, or who are first in their family to get a college degree. It has a particular strength in professional programs like physician's assistant or nursing. The students are eager and committed, and intellectually, they're certainly no slouches. But they were obviously different from the MIT students he had taught before.

Once a student in his Le Moyne class was making a class presentation and happened to mention a certain principle from Aristotle. At that, another student let out a loud groan followed by a pronounced roll of the eyes. "She must not care for philosophy," Br. Guy thought.

But then the student sitting next to her leaped from his desk, grabbed her, and gently laid her limp body on the floor. Another pulled out his cell phone and called campus patrol, describing the kind of seizure she had had, and reporting the building and classroom where they were. Within five minutes, medical help was on hand.

Seizure? "I just thought she was being rude," Br. Guy reflected. And then he realized, "If this had been a classroom full of MIT students like me, that poor woman could have been dead before anyone would have noticed what had happened... much less would have known what to do."

Chris Graney had a similar experience when he was a young professor and was teaching a technical physics class at a satellite campus of his community college, located in a small town in Kentucky. This was not a wealthy place—the "campus" was in a century-old building that had been poorly renovated and was sufficiently decrepit that a professor could find water running out from under the wall by the whiteboard at which he was lecturing...from a toilet overflowing in the adjacent bathroom! *Ugh!* Not the place where the "best and brightest" hang out, right?

Well...

As a "fun project," Prof. Graney assigned his physics students to build catapults that would throw vegetables as their projectiles. There would be a competition near the end of the semester. He envisioned modest devices made of wood and PVC pipe.

But he underestimated his students. Most of them worked in local industries and had skills he did not consider. They convinced their employers to loan or give them costly materials. They got out welders, torches, and other tools. Unbeknownst to their professor, they proceeded to put their skills and their physics knowledge to work in an arms race that resulted in large, truck-mounted engines of war that, in a different era (this was prior to the terror attacks of September 11, 2001) might have attracted the attention of the authorities.

As it was, they attracted the attention of the local community when the students were testing them out. When one of those engines malfunctioned in spectacular fashion outside a local factory, disrupting work and coming very close to seriously injuring people, a townsperson called Chris up and said, "Professor Graney, you need to know what your students are doing." He shut down the competition. (Which then provoked an outcry because everyone was having so much fun, but that is another story. In the end, the students got to demonstrate what they could do, and everyone lived to tell tales.)

The history of humanity is full of stories of people who were not expected to be among the best and the brightest in fact being the best and the brightest. Consider another guy from Kentucky, who grew up not at all wealthy. Abraham Lincoln was his name.

So, given all this, why would anyone think that we could measure and evaluate what people can do, that we could "scientifically" determine who is "superior," when it comes to broad concepts like intelligence?

And yet it still happens. We seem to have a desire to rank ourselves and others based on "intelligence." Of all the criteria that differentiate one person from another, intelligence in our modern culture has taken on a disproportionate importance. That desire has a profound consequence on how we deal with each other and how we evaluate ourselves.

The desire to see yourself as smarter than average—and the fear of looking like you're only average or, worse, less intelligent than average—can be seen everywhere. It can be seen in schoolyard taunts, of course, but it can also be seen in the form of a broad skepticism—of which vaccine skepticism is but a prominent example—that says that the really smart person does not fall for the stuff that everyone else—all those sheep—falls for. This skepticism not only erodes our trust in authority but also sets up a universal relativism that undermines the idea that anyone can ever be able to know the truth.

Skepticism would seem to have a solid basis in science. Galileo is a hero of modern science and the scientific method, and rightly so; and he is seen as a very intelligent guy for being a famous skeptic of the received wisdom of his times. His famous principle expressed in *The Assayer* (his treatise on the philosophy of science) is that the evidence of observation and experiment counts more than any number of authoritative pronouncements from the sages of the ages.

And yet, one of the ironic insights that J. L. Heilbron makes in his recent biography of Galileo is why the famous scientist was so resistant to authority. Heilbron argues that Galileo rejected authority precisely on the authority of his father and his teachers. Galileo was a rebel against what was being taught, precisely because he had been taught to be so!

Rebellion against authority is, of course, a common behavior in adolescents, who are testing and defining the boundaries of their autonomy. Remember the slogan often seen on T-shirts and political-style buttons: "Question authority!" (Of course, an adolescent who wanted to be an even greater contrarian against the contrarians would be free to respond, "Says who?")

WHEN SCIENCE GOES WRONG

The type of skepticism that puts experiments above authority has been a hallmark of modern science since its beginnings in Galileo's time. But in the public mind, it has been conflated with the vaccine skepticism that we experienced during the COVID-19 pandemic: we intelligent, free-thinking people who question the vaccine-promoting authorities are just following in the footsteps of Galileo! (Such skepticism was around long before COVID-19—and doubtless it will outlive this pandemic. Edward Jenner himself had to fight it when he devised the first smallpox vaccine in 1796.)

But the skepticism seen with the vaccines is not Galileo's skepticism of wanting to trust only experiment—to trust reality, to trust truth—over authoritative pronouncements. (And let's not just credit such skepticism to Galileo; Locher and Scheiner, Riccioli, and others were themselves desiring to test ideas against reality). Skepticism today often seems to come from social or political motivations. It's not a desire to run some experiments, publish the results so others can replicate them, and thus put authoritative pronouncements to the test. No, it's a tribal marker, a way of saying "I am one of *these* people, one of the *intelligent* people who think for themselves—not one of *those* people, one of the sheep." (Note that when people tie acceptance of the vaccine to the acceptance of "science" itself, they can wind up having vaccine skepticism lead to science skepticism, making "science" itself a tribal marker. And that doesn't do science any good.)

You can find vaccine skeptics across all populations and demographic groups, but it is an attitude that is especially strong among certain religious groups. Writing in the *New York Times* in 2021, the Anglican priest Tish Harrison Warren suggested that this split was evidence of the more general division perceived in our culture between science and religion. She wrote, "These past two years have exposed how the science vs. faith discourse isn't an abstract ideological debate but a false dichotomy that has disastrous real-world consequences." Her insight came out of research showing that Evangelical Christians in the United States were one of the populations that are the least vaccinated against the coronavirus. The implication was that a distrust of science in this community, reflected in their distrust of vaccines, was tied to their perceived need to choose between science and faith—a choice promoted by the language of nineteenth-century scientists like Nott and Pouchet.

But of course, this distrust can be found in religious groups well beyond the Evangelicals. Many Catholics have expressed similar views, even in the face of strong urgings from the Vatican and Pope Francis himself that vaccination was not only a moral way to protect your own life, but an essential step in safeguarding the health and safety of the larger community. Getting vaccinated was not just encouraged; if you worked at the Vatican, like we do at the Vatican Observatory, during the height of the COVID-19 pandemic, it was the law. You could not set foot on Vatican territory without a "green pass" that indicated that you had been vaccinated.

There's a further irony, of course, seen in some of the vaccine skeptics. After they announced that they were too clever to be fooled by the experts, some started self-dosing with utterly inappropriate and dangerous drugs that they happened to read about on the internet. The same skeptics who urged us not to be sheep, tried to cure themselves from COVID-19 by taking drugs meant for sheep.

How does this happen? Why would people who regard themselves as intelligent reject the best science of the day and instead trust their health to something they found on the internet? But then, why would anyone reject organized religion with a long history of careful, systemic thought about God and human beings in favor of a philosophy you can read on a T-shirt or a bumper sticker?

It does not happen because of a lack of intelligence on the part of skeptics. Perhaps it happens because, in our society, skepticism of authority runs alongside a desire for certainty that leads to an excessive credulity in science. The two desires are, of course, antithetical. You cannot at the same time demand perfect truth while also rejecting any authority that would claim to lead you toward that truth.

What results instead when our brains are faced with these two diametrically opposite desires is that we wind up squirting off sideways. We reject "officially sanctioned" authority in favor of a secret source of knowledge available only to a hidden few. And even though something that can be found on a web page is, by definition, available to everyone who can get on the internet, the experience of discovering it by yourself on your own personal computer in the confines of your bedroom creates the illusion that this is a private and hidden discovery, open to those intelligent enough to find it… one that by its hidden nature appears to have value beyond that received via more public media.

And, by the way, one that is also easy! If you were a complete skeptic, you *could*, after all, reject all of science and all the technology that comes from science, and reject all of organized religion, and all of human thought in general, and go live in a cave and start to redevelop it all from scratch, by dropping rocks and looking at water and heating dirt in fire and rediscovering everything for yourself. But no skeptic does that. Private and hidden discovery via internet is so much easier!

The temptation to easy private discovery is one we should recognize. It is the allure of Gnosticism, a desire to embrace "secret knowledge." It was a prominent movement at the time of the church fathers in the second and third centuries. Well before then, you can see it in the esoteric Eleusinian rites of ancient Greece. And after all, "I'll tell you secret knowledge that God doesn't want you to have" was the temptation of the snake in the Garden. And this secret knowledge would come easily; Adam and Eve only had to eat an apple, not build their own Garden.

It is instructive to see how this desire for secret knowledge can manifest itself even among those who might legitimately be thought to be highly knowledgeable already. People like scientists (like the authors of this book!), engineers, medical doctors, and others highly educated in fields of science, technology, engineering, and mathematics (STEM) are particularly tempted to think of themselves as smarter than the rest of the world. That's not so surprising—that attitude is what they are taught. (Recall Br. Guy's snide comments in his thesis; had they earned him a sharp reprimand, he would have removed them.)

All too often, such people can be confident to the point of arrogance about their intellectual ability, their ability to work things out on their own. They are, after all, highly trained at their own work, and they can sometimes extrapolate their experience with their own abilities in science to a perceived superiority in the knowledge of all subjects.

Just look at how the Cambridge physicist Stephen Hawking would philosophize about God and the origin of the universe, while insisting that he was not a philosopher...implying that, since he was a scientist, he was better than a mere philosopher. Likewise, the astronomer Neil deGrasse Tyson at the American Museum of Natural History appears to have an opinion about nearly everything, and an urge to share that opinion on social media, no matter how far the topic is from his realm of expertise.

Some are especially vulnerable to a particular variant of this sense of privilege. While scientists who are involved in published research get their sense of value from how much their ideas are accepted and cited by other scientists (and so they tend to be sensitive to what other people, or at least other scientists, think of them), the worth of others in the STEM

119

fields can proceed from less social means. If engineers make good widgets or doctors save lives in the hospital, they'll get hired and they'll get promoted regardless of how poorly their other opinions might be accepted by the broader community.

Furthermore, these talented people can often be surrounded at their work by bosses who don't really understand what they do. Engineers, for example, are used to thinking of themselves as "the smartest people in the room" precisely because they have to share that room with the non-engineers—with the "suits"—who may have no understanding of the gizmos their company sells. And in some cases, those "smartest people in the room" can be right! The loss of the space shuttles *Challenger* and *Columbia*, for example, had much to do with the "suits" at NASA not listening to the reality the engineers were describing.

Since engineers, and others in the STEM world, are not inhibited by social pressures in this way, some may feel free to adopt beliefs, including skeptical ones, that the rest of the world would find absurd. The fact that hardly anyone else seems to share their beliefs in some specific bizarre idea doesn't surprise them; instead, it just confirms their conviction that they are smarter than everyone else.

Indeed, what's the point of being the smartest person in the room if all you do is just agree with everyone else? With that attitude, you almost have to be a contrarian. This makes such folk easy prey for the peddlers of modern forms of Gnosticism—from UFOs and the "face on Mars" to faddish diets and strange new religions, none of which stand up to Galileo's form of skepticism. The crazy thing is that, if they could convince everyone else to come over to their side, they'd probably change their own minds to stay in the elite minority!

There's a particularly dangerous effect that can occur once holding fringe beliefs does come to place a cost on the believer. Maybe eventually you lose your social status, or maybe you lose your job, because your ideas are so out of line. In a case like that, this "persecution" that you think you're suffering can turn your unorthodox belief into a marker of self-identity. If your beliefs come at a high personal cost, then you become so invested in your own peculiar belief that you can't ever admit that you were wrong. To abandon that belief in favor of what everybody else thinks would make you feel like you were abandoning your very self.

Notice that while this tendency might be particularly acute among certain people in STEM fields, it is a trait found widely in our society. Again, ironically, our desire to maintain our personal identity in the face of a hostile culture is something that we learn from that very same culture. Just think of the famous athlete who claims that he will "do his own research" to decide if the COVID-19 vaccine is efficacious (by searching the internet, not by setting up a lab and doing experiments). This attitude reinforces his sense of "stardom," that he's superior to everyone else in the room. (More often than not, this same athlete is someone who also has a hard time listening to his coaches.)

The urge toward such an attitude has serious consequences to our society. People demanding perfect truth, rejecting any authority that would claim to lead them toward that truth, yet being unwilling to do the hard work needed to get to the truth or to at least contribute to the search for the truth, has led to the "post truth" age: what is true is only what agrees with my biases, with my tribe, with my identity, with what I want to hear (and in the internet age, I can always find, easily, what I want to hear). Those who think otherwise will seem to me as lacking in intelligence or, worse, being malevolent.

Rather than heaping scorn on those who fall prey to such urges, maybe we should look at the origin of these ideas.

If we assume that scientists—or authors of the "secret" websites, if you prefer—deserve to be followed because they are more intelligent than the rest of us, then implicitly, we equate "more intelligent" with "better." That was the root temptation toward much of eugenics, and it is at the root of the temptation to Gnosticism: letting your sense of self-worth come from thinking that you are more intelligent than the average person, that you are the "smartest person in the room."

But consider the unspoken assumption in this evaluation, the identification of "being smarter" as a marker of personal superiority.

That marker is not self-evident. Consider the legend of John Henry defeating the steam drill. The man who designed the steam drill thought he was mighty smart, the story goes. But he was not a more superior hammer swinger than John Henry. Maybe he was not a superior husband, or son, or father, or friend, either. Maybe, even, he was not more talented at design. (John Henry probably did not have much chance to work on steam drill design.)

That marker sure doesn't show up in Christian belief. Matthew 11:25, for example, quotes Jesus saying, "I thank you, Father, Lord of heaven and earth, because you have hidden these things from the wise and the intelligent and have revealed them to infants." In 1 Corinthians 1:17—2:7, Paul insists that the wisdom of the gospel looks very different from what the world considers wise.

And consider whom it is we acknowledge as saints and heroes. There were many learned theologians in nineteenth-century Belgium and France (most of them at each other's throats), but the saints of that era were people like Bernadette of Lourdes; Antoine-Frédéric Ozanam, who founded the Society of St. Vincent de Paul; and Thérèse, the Little Flower. They were not concerned about scoring theological points; they were concerned about loving God. Their concern warns us of the deeper and more subtle issue present in this chapter, one that goes beyond the cult of intelligence: the temptation to hold up *any* person, even a Serena Williams or an Abraham Lincoln, as superior and more worthy in some broader sense than others. Instead, what we should be holding up is the love of God.

This is not to demean intelligence or any other ability, and it is not to demean theology or theologians. After all, we are professional astronomers; we think we're intelligent. But it does mean that intelligence cannot be correlated with "worth" any more than strength can be. The value of whatever intelligence, education, or even wisdom that we have does not lie in those attributes themselves. Whatever we do has value only insofar as it is a form of praise to our Creator.

We all have our own God-given talents and abilities, whether they are academic or something else. It is certainly legitimate to measure how people differ from one another, just as it is great fun to test our athletic abilities or participate in other sorts of contests. But our worth does not derive from the results of such tests. Any science that seeks to measure our *worth* by measuring one trait or another is science gone wrong.

Engaging our abilities makes us more authentically the persons whom God created us to be, and thus able to encounter God more fully, each in our own way. For the authors of this book, astronomy happens to be the playing field where we have been given an opportunity to come to know God. Others find God in places that we cannot reach. That is how we—as children of God, created in the image of God, and thus of immeasurable worth—find God in all things, and do all things for the greater glory of God.

Conclusion

When Faith Goes Wrong

So far, we've told stories from the history of science about how science can go wrong. We've outlined specific themes, ways where the very nature of how we do science can lead to error, even as it ultimately leads us closer to the truth.

But of course, those ways that science goes wrong are not only limited to science.

Extrapolation? Consider how we might think we have been able to get by so far without believing in God, and likewise we don't seem to need God right now, today; and so we happily extrapolate to assume that there will never be a need to ever think about God. The casual agnosticism of our culture is firmly founded on this sort of extrapolation.

Mashups? The confusion of biblical teachings with Greek philosophy in the early church led to as many heresies as it did to insights. Throw in modern philosophy, and the opportunities for mischief today are rife, limited only by the imagination of the modern armchair philosopher, who can, and will, mashup "Jedi religion" from *Star Wars* with the "multiverse" and something found online about druids to produce who knows what....

Confirmation bias? St. Paul warns about this in his Second Letter to Timothy when he describes those who "have an itch to hear what they want to hear" (see 2 Timothy 4:3). The songwriter Paul Simon echoed that in "The Boxer": "A man hears what he wants to hear and disregards the rest." This approach can be the temptation to let our faith—or at least the teachers of our faith whom we choose to listen to—teach us only a comfortable confirmation of who we already are and what we already want to believe. Or it can be the temptation to see our faith only with the eyes of fear and hear only condemnation and rejection.

Failure of imagination? Biblical literalism is one obvious place where we treat words as prescriptions rather than as spurs to bring us closer to God. In the same way, though, ignoring the teachings of Scripture out of hand rather than taking them seriously is also a result of failing to imagine how they could possibly apply to us and our own time and situation.

The cult of being superior? How often are we tempted to divide our church into "we few," as a small, persecuted flock who truly understand Jesus, unlike those blind and rigid fundamentalists, or those liberal theologians, or those darned bishops, who keep trying to force fetters on our faith, or those "cafeteria Catholics," who ignore all the rules. We'd be better off without them! The desire to purge our church of "the others" who can't possibly be close to God, much less have anything important to teach us, carries a whiff of intellectual eugenics. It is tied to our desire to judge ourselves as the "holiest person in the room."

Again, consider what we have learned from the COVID-19 pandemic and the way people reacted to it. "Follow the science!" was the rallying cry of people who promoted COVID-19 vaccination. And, as we noted, it was a slogan that clearly did not work. In other words, it didn't convince anyone to change their views of vaccination. (Of course, if the purpose of the slogan was to make you feel superior to the nonscientific rabble, it worked just fine!) Worse, while we are all in favor of vaccinations, the wording of the motto, "follow the science," is emblematic of a misleading conception of science that leaves science open to attack.

The authors of this book are scientists. We have no trouble putting trust in science, even as we recognize that it is not infallible. We love it even as we know it can go wrong. But to trust in science is not the same as to "follow" the science. We are also persons of faith, and we recognize that the phrase "follow the science" can sound an awful lot like a challenge to the invitation of Jesus, "Follow me"; as a rival answer to Peter's plaint in John's Gospel, "Lord, to whom can we go?" (John 6:68). If you hear it that way, the vaccine—and the science—becomes a substitute for Jesus.

"Follow the science" carries not merely the idea that science is a trustworthy guide to truth; it also suggests that science is the *only* such trustworthy guide. And plenty of people do more than suggest that—they insist that it is the only such guide. When you treat science as the source of truth, you set it up as a rival to "the way, the truth, and the light." And from the idea that science is the only trustworthy guide you can easily extrapolate to the idea that the authority of science is all but infallible. Then, when science fails—the whole point of the stories in this book; it happens so often!—when science does not live up to an exaggerated reliability as the truth, then that failure winds up feeding the very skepticism we wanted to defuse.

But the issue goes deeper than that. The fight over "follow the science" is really a fight over the reliability of authority, in general. To treat scientists as members of a kind of priesthood of truth is a questionable tactic, especially in a society where actual priests are viewed with suspicion!

At the end of the day, both those who promote science, and those who disdain it, are looking for certainty in an uncertain universe. It is an almost rigid intolerance of error. We yearn for a world of black and white distinctions, where "failure is not an option."

The irony is that, in science, failure isn't an option; it's a requirement.

As our stories have shown, science itself is actually based on doubt and error...learning when to doubt the current thinking, and learning how to analyze and learn from our error. It is essential to know that you don't know. Knowing our ignorance is what motivates us to work to know better and not be satisfied with what we knew already.

Once again, notice the parallel with our faith lives. Knowing that our relationship with God is not perfect is an essential step toward growing closer to God. (Knowing that God's love for us doesn't depend on us being perfect is another essential step!)

But there's something even deeper going on here. Science is not merely sometimes incomplete; it is, by design, always incomplete. It is precisely when the scientific work is done correctly and it advances the field that it becomes obsolete. Indeed, a sign of a successful piece of science is that it pushes the field beyond the understanding that was assumed when the work began. Once scientific knowledge is advanced, the original work itself is no longer current. Science is in the business of making itself obsolete. In this sense, science is very different from philosophy; you might study philosophy by reading your grandfather's copy of the works of Aristotle, but you would never study biology from your grandfather's biology textbook.

The astonishing thing is that the stories we've told here of science gone wrong are mostly stories of science going right: science advancing. Aristotle understood that things on Earth obeyed "laws." Even though the laws he proposed were eventually found wanting, the very idea that there exist laws of nature is a cornerstone of science. That was a major advance, fundamental to all that we've been able to understand about how the physical universe works. And it was an advance that the Book of Genesis anticipated, long before Aristotle.

Columbus risked his life—and those of his crews—on a false idea of the size and nature of the "high seas." But he discovered America in the process. And when the mere existence of the Americas disproved the very idea Columbus had depended on, that freed Copernicus fifty years later from an old cosmology, allowing him to try out a new way of imagining the Earth and the heavens.

The arguments of Tycho Brahe and his followers against a moving Earth seemed irrefutable in their time. And yet, while we now know they were wrong, the individual arguments were correct, and connected to important advances in physics. Trying to figure out where they went wrong when applied to Brahe's cosmology led to new discoveries about the motions of bodies and the nature of light.

For hundreds of years, from the invention of the telescope to the end of the nineteenth century, astronomers managed to observe and study the moons of Jupiter without ever having a clue as to what they were actually looking at. The flaw was not in their data, but in the assumption that certain questions were "not properly of astronomical interest." Finally, when Pickering did ask the right questions, his conclusion that the moons of Jupiter were made of white sand certainly fit his data. His only problem was a lack of imagination that limited his ability to see other explanations.

Eugenics was a case of putting too much faith in what seemed to be good cutting-edge science—science applied to measuring people. But it failed in no small part because of the unspoken ideas about the nature of "superiority" carried by the scientists involved. Applying science and measurement to people is not inherently bad. If some people are not thriving, and science can help us understand why, that is good. But the starting point must be that all people are God's children and of worth beyond measure, and in that way "created equal." That bit of truth, which comes from outside science, is the starting point that ensures that our tendency toward a cult of superiority and intelligence does not lead our science toward terrible mistakes.

We need to grapple with mistakes, with the fact that science goes wrong, with scientific ideas becoming obsolete, with science's incompleteness, because we all want science. Consider how, as you read this book, you are probably not sitting in a cave, trying to build all human knowledge from scratch on your own. Rather, you are probably surrounded by the technical products of science that make your life better than it would be in that cave.

When I'm sick and go to a doctor, I want medicine to make my life better, to solve my problem. I am not there for some philosophical debate about the imperfection of medicine. The doctor probably will be able to help—that's why doctors are so valued in modern society. But medicine is never perfect, and practitioners of medicine even less so. Doctors can't cure everything; indeed, they're human, and sometimes they make mistakes. Yet if I am ill, I would still rather see one of those imperfect doctors than stay at home, in the cave, and hope for the best (or try to cure myself based on something I read on the internet).

It is the same with science generally. Science going wrong, making mistakes, is still valuable.

A need to be open to mistakes is a lesson that goes beyond the world of science. To give a trivial example: when Br. Guy was a student at MIT, he was on the collegiate sailing team; and for all the times he went sailing on the Charles River, he never once capsized his boat. But he also never won a race. The two are related: he never pushed his small dinghy to find the limits of how far and fast it could go before it capsized.

Learning to fail is difficult. It requires gauging the impossible balance of determining when to keep pushing at an idea that just needs a little more work before it works and knowing when it is time to admit you're wrong and look for a different approach. Tycho Brahe resisted the new idea of a moving Earth; he was a remarkable observer of the heavens, but he was wrong. The Catholic apologist G. K. Chesterton strongly resisted the new eugenics of H. G. Wells, and instead argued for the traditional sanctity of human life against interpretations of Darwin's ideas that Chesterton described as "survival of the nastiest." Chesterton was right, both scientifically and morally. "New" is neither necessarily right nor necessarily wrong. But, as any poker player knows, there is no simple calculus that can make the decision for you of when to hold and when to fold.

The problem is not even one as simple as seeking more data to resolve the issue. The issue may well be that the idea in question requires a complete change in the way you understand the data. Consider those astronomers like Locher and Scheiner, and even Kepler, who followed Brahe in his ideas about stars being strange bodies larger than Earth's orbit. Those astronomers could have collected all the data on the sizes of stars that they wanted, but until someone figured out that the little disks of light that they saw when looking at the stars were an illusion, more data would not have helped them. Science is not merely a description, however accurate, of what we see happening in the natural world. It is also a quest to understand why things happen the way they do. To be able to predict what will happen, to "get the right answer," is not the goal in and of itself; merely, it is a way of judging the strength of our current level of understanding.

Ptolemy and Kepler, both of whom we have met in this book, can provide another example to illustrate this. Both, in addition to doing the various things discussed in the previous chapters, tried to describe with geometry the motions of planets through the constellations of the night sky. In a sense, Ptolemy got the "right answer." He used a system of circles moving on circles. In theory, his system can perfectly match any possible planetary path—if you allow yourself to add enough circles to the calculation. (A wag on YouTube once made a Ptolemaic construction that would draw Homer Simpson.) By contrast, Kepler used single ellipses that cannot themselves account for minor planetary perturbations, and so they are uncertain—only approximately correct. But Ptolemy's calculations were sterile; they did not lead to any deeper insight into the nature of why the planets moved the way they did. Indeed, it's doubtful if Ptolemy even asked that question. Kepler's ellipses, on the other hand, helped Newton to derive his law of gravity. They are what astronomers use today.

The difficulty is that accepting such uncertainty means also accepting the risk that comes from attempting the uncertain. You cannot win races without risking a capsize. But to capsize is a real, unpleasant, and nonnegligible risk. Yet sometimes, when you are attempting the uncertain, there are people in the boat with you—like when your science is not about the nature of the seas, but about the nature of human beings. The risk calculation changes.

There is a parallel here with faith. We start out teaching our children faith like we teach them science—you need to get the "right answers"; know the Lord 's Prayer, know the Creed. Those are good things, like knowing how to use Newton's ideas about momentum and gravity to solve an orbital problem and get the answer in the back of the book. And the Lord's Prayer and the Creed won't capsize people's boats.

But in the real world, things are not so clear-cut and certain, both in faith and science. The popular religious writer Anne Lamott, in her book *Plan B: Further Thoughts on Faith*, speaks to certainty, and risk, and knowing the answers: "The opposite of faith is not doubt; the opposite of faith is certainty." If we didn't have doubts, we wouldn't need faith. And like in science, we need to keep looking to the truth, looking for God and not being satisfied with just accepting, or rejecting, whatever we had learned when we were children. Paul Tillich wrote in *Dynamics of Faith* that the role of doubt in faith is "the doubt which accompanies every risk. It is not the permanent doubt of the scientist, and it is not the transitory doubt of the skeptic, but it is the doubt of him who is ultimately concerned about a concrete content. One could call it the existential doubt....It is aware of the element of insecurity in every existential truth." He also notes that, "Serious doubt is confirmation of faith. It indicates the seriousness of the concern, its unconditional character."

Accepting doubt, accepting the inevitability of error, also means accepting a tolerance for other people even when they have been wrong. We can still enjoy the stories of H. G. Wells (incidentally, he was a great friend of Chesterton); we can still admire much that Oliver Wendell Holmes did as a chief justice; we can still use Alexander Graham Bell's telephone...even as we abhor their views on eugenics. We can accept that heroes sometimes are also sinners, even serious sinners. Maybe we can even admit that we are sinners, too.

Much as science is a search for truth that does not guarantee that things will not go wrong, religion is a search for truth that does not give a certain formula that guarantees salvation. Such a formalism would imply that salvation can be earned by our own behavior, by following a formula, rather than received as the unearned gift of a loving God. But religion can teach about the gift that has been offered and give us a way in which we can express our acceptance of that gift.

Seeing how the search for truth plays an essential role in both science and faith, you can appreciate that science and religion seem to be in conflict only if you neglect the role of uncertainty in each of them. You only can see them in conflict if you think of both as closed books of rules, books of facts, each demanding infallible credulity. Certainty is not religion; it's presumption—you think you know it as well as God. Certainty is not science; it's scientism—you think science is god, or at least as close to an all-knowing, all-powerful god as there can be.

Science does not give perfect truth. Ever-refined experiments or theories might result in more precise descriptions of nature, but an essential lesson for every student of science is to learn the difference between precision and accuracy. A highly precise measurement can nonetheless be subject to a significant systematic error. No yardstick is perfect.

And no matter how good our science is, it will always be subject not only to the systematic inaccuracies of our instruments—like with the star sizes—but also to our human tendencies to force the data to fit our preconceptions—like with the Coriolis effect, or with eugenics. Any understanding that thinks of itself as perfect is dead; it will never seek to understand further. When we see that things go wrong, by contrast, then not only do we seek to understand further, but the more we do grow to understand, the more amusing our earlier conceptions will seem to be!

Science, like faith, can provide insights into how to see and recognize truth. And it can tell us the odds of success for a given formulation of that truth. We trust a vaccine not because it is perfect, but because it vastly improves one's odds of not getting sick. The long-term effects of a vaccine cannot be known until, obviously, a long time has passed; but meanwhile, the short-term effects of not getting vaccinated are all too obvious. Recall the family we talked about at the beginning of this book; Nancy, Julie, and her children lost a beloved husband and father.

Reflecting on both that death and the nature of our own scientific work, we uncover a bigger connection behind what we do and why we do it. Faith and science are ultimately about love: the people we love; the Creator we love; the work we do that we love.

Again, the authors of this book are scientists. We love science. We love doing science. But anyone's lifetime résumé of scientific papers must include many that turned out to be mistaken, and many more that are now obsolete. We still love the science, even when we were wrong. And we should be proud of the obsolete papers; that means we were working in the right place, a place that was so interesting to so many people that they worked to move us from what we thought we knew. Our science was not, and is not, perfect. Hurrah for science!

Love does not demand perfection. Love admits error, admits doubt, admits mistakes...both on our parts and on the part of those we love. If we demand perfection of others, we can never admit to imperfections in ourselves. And as we have seen in the world of science, we cannot grow if we do not accept that we need to grow. That is the nature of love. That is central to God's love of us.

Further Reading

Introduction

Consolmagno, Guy. "Covid, fede e fallibilità della scienza." *La Civiltà Cattolica*, January 15, 2022. "Covid, Faith, and the Fallibility of Science." *La Civiltà Cattolica* (English edition).

―――――. "Trust the Science." *The Tablet*, January 29, 2022. This article was a discussion of the reactions to the original *Civiltà Cattolica* article. Many of the points in the preface and conclusion were originally raised in this article.

Chapter 1

Consolmagno, Guy. *Brother Astronomer: Adventures of a Vatican Scientist*. New York: McGraw-Hill, 2000. Here, readers will find material pertaining not only to chapter 1 but also chapters 4 and 5—material on topics from Eriugena to the equations Br. Guy used in his calculations regarding Europa.

Consolmagno, Guy, and Christopher M. Graney. "The Galileo Myth." *America*, September 18, 2020. A short discussion touching on several of the main ideas presented in our book.

Graney, Christopher M. *Setting Aside All Authority: Giovanni Battista Riccioli and the Science against Copernicus in the Age of Galileo*. Notre Dame, IN: University of Notre Dame Press, 2015. Chapters 1 and 3 rely greatly on material from this book.

Scheiner, Christoph, and Johann Georg Locher. "Mathematical Dis-
quisitions." In *Mathematical Disquisitions: The Booklet of
Theses Immortalized by Galileo.* Translated by Christopher M.
Graney. Notre Dame, IN: University of Notre Dame Press, 2017.
Fr. Scheiner and Mr. Locher appear in several of our chapters,
and here is where to learn more about what they had to say.

Chapter 2

Starkey, Lindsay J. *Encountering Water in Early Modern Europe and
Beyond: Redefining the Universe through Natural Philosophy,
Religious Reformations and Sea Voyaging.* Amsterdam: Amsterdam University Press, 2020. For the reader who wants even
more on the material discussed in chapter 2.

Wootton, David. *The Invention of Science: A New History of the Scientific Revolution.* New York: Allen Lane/Penguin Random House,
2015. We were first introduced to the Two Spheres Theory by
Wootton's chapter 4, "Planet Earth."

Chapter 3

Consolmagno, Guy, and Christopher M. Graney. "Spin off: The Surprising History of the Coriolis Effect and the Jesuits who investigated
it." *Catholic Historical Review* 109, no. 2 (2023): 302–20. A more
detailed and scholarly discussion of Jesuits and the Coriolis
effect.

Graney, Christopher M. "Wide of the Mark by 100 yards: Textbooks
and the Falklands Coriolis Myth." *Physics Today-Online.* Febru-
ary 2, 2022. https://physicstoday.scitation.org/do/10.1063/
pt.6.3.20220202b/full/.

Chapter 4

Chinnici, Ileana. *Decoding the Stars: A Biography of Angelo Secchi,
Jesuit and Scientist.* Leiden: Brill, 2019.

Consolmagno, Guy, and Christopher M. Graney. "Slipping on Jupiter's Icy Moons." *Sky & Telescope* (October 2022): 34–40. This article tells the same story as our chapter 4, but for an audience of astronomers.

Glatz, Carol. "Mapping with the Stars: Nuns Instrumental in Vatican Celestial Survey." *National Catholic Reporter-Online.* April 30, 2016. https://www.ncronline.org/blogs/eco-catholic/mapping-stars-nuns-instrumental-vatican-celestial-survey. More on the "computers" discussed in chapter 4.

Chapter 5

Consolmagno, Guy. *My Theology: Finding God in the Universe.* London: Darton, Longman and Todd, 2021. This book includes an extended discussion of how science is the work of a community, not a lone genius, "the smartest guy in the room."

Heilbron, John L. *Galileo.* New York: Oxford University Press, 2010. This book has a wonderful description of Galileo's education, including his reliance on authority...and his own issues arising from his desire to be thought of as "the smartest guy in the room."

Kelves, Daniel J. *In the Name of Eugenics.* New York: Alfred A. Knopf, 1985. A history of the eugenics movement; the preface to the 1995 edition notes how modern advances in genetics may once again tempt people toward embracing this false hope of human "improvement."

Kindi, Ibram X. *Stamped from the Beginning: The Definitive History of Racist Ideas in America.* New York: Nation Books, 2016. Kindi began this book as a history of science and racism.

Livingstone, David N. *Adam's Ancestors: Race, Religion and the Politics of Human Origins.* Baltimore, MD: Johns Hopkins University Press, 2008.

———. *Dealing with Darwin: Place, Politics, and Rhetoric in Religious Engagements with Evolution.* Baltimore, MD: Johns Hopkins University Press, 2014.

Index

AAAS. *See* American Association for the Advancement of Science

abilities of differing groups (and judgments about them), 110, 112, 119, 123

abortion (and prenatal testing), 106

Adam, 119; sons of, 102–3

Agassiz, Louis, 103

air (Aristotelian element). *See* elements

air (atmospheric): Coriolis Effect and weather, 65, 70; and densities, 92; in Galileo's discussions, 56–57; refractive effects of, 43–46

albedo, 82, 87, 93–94

America (continents of), and Copernicus, 42–43, 128

American Association for the Advancement of Science (AAAS), 102–3; 1850 meeting of, 102–3; its journal *Science*, 102, 104

ammonia (in planetary atmospheres), 83

angels (ranks of), 10–11

Apollo moon landings (supposedly faked), 77

Aquinas, St. Thomas, 14, 47, 53, 60

arc minute and arc second, 86

Aristarchus, 12–13

Aristotle, xvi; adapted to Christian ideas, 23; disputes about, 12; as an example of obsolete but significant scientific ideas, 127; ideas about the universe, 4–7, 10, 25–31, 74–75; ideas of and the Bible, 46, 52–54; and the universe functioning according to rules, 27–29. *See also* elements

Aryabhata, 5–6, 49–50

Asimov, Isaac, xix

astrology, 6

astronomers: views of and attitudes of, 19, 91–92, 97–98, 123; work of, xvii

78; Pius X, 89; Pius XI, 90;
Pius XII, 47–48
"positive eugenics." *See*
eugenics
"post-truth" age or society,
75–78, 121
Pouchet, Georges, 107–9, 117
precision. *See* measurement
prenatal testing, 106
pressure (in weather), 65, 70
priesthood of truth, 126
projectiles, 60, 62–63, 69, 74,
113–14. *See also* cannon and
cannonballs
proofs for the existence of God.
See God
Protestant reformers, 60
providence of God, 8, 37
pseudo-science. *See* eugenics
Ptolemy, 6–14, 23, 53, 63, 99,
130–31; and Genesis, 7;
Ptolemaic construction of
Homer Simpson, 131

quintessence (Aristotelian
element). *See* elements

radioactivity, 80–81
rainbow (spectrum), 83
refraction. *See under* elements
relativism, 75, 115
religion, ix–x, 46, 120, 131,
133; organized, 116–18; and
science, x, 7, 36, 55, 100, 126,
132; and truth, 107, 132
Riccioli, Giovanni Battista, SJ
(Coriolis Effect), 63–65,

67–69, 73–74, 116; *New
Almagest*, 63, 69
rock, 40, 83, 92, 118; composes
much of Earth, 5, 43, 50, 59;
in Jovian moons, 79–85, 96
rotation, 48, 73; of Earth, 26,
40, 43–45, 48, 50, 53, 57–58,
60–71, 75–76; of the sun, 48

Sagan, Carl: and Guy
Consolmagno, 96–97; *Pale
Blue Dot* discourse, 9, 11
St. Ignatius of Loyola Church /
observatory (Rome),
83–84, 86
saints, 7–8, 10, 14–15, 23, 47,
53, 108, 122, 124
salt, xvi, 49
salvation, 132
sand, 28; moons made of,
94–95, 98–99, 128
Saturn, 21, 84, 97
Scheiner, Christoph, SJ, 44, 59,
116, 130; on Jovian moons,
94; on orbiting as falling,
61–62, 88; and the rotation
of Earth, 60–62, 64, 73, 76
Schott, Gaspar, SJ, 32–33
science fiction, 22, 24, 104
Science (journal). *See* American
Association for the
Advancement of Science
science, 1: crackpot, xviii,
108; and Genesis making
possible, 3–4, 76; going
wrong, i–xx, 1–134;
incomplete and changing,

The authors thank Angela Elliott and Christina Graney who, out of the goodness of their hearts, read this book in its entirety to help us catch errors and improve our wording, and helped build the index.